The American South

The American South

SEVEN BOOKS SUGGESTED
FOR REPRINTING BY
C. VANN WOODWARD

G. W. Dyer
Democracy in the South Before the Civil War. 1905

D. R. Hundley
Social Relations in Our Southern States. 1860

Charles H. Otken
The Ills of the South, Or, Related Causes Hostile to the General Prosperity of the Southern People. 1894

Robert Royal Russel
Economic Aspects of Southern Sectionalism, 1840–1861. 1923

Robert Somers
The Southern States Since the War, 1870–1. 1871

D. Augustus Straker
The New South Investigated. 1888

Richard Taylor
Destruction and Reconstruction: Personal Experiences of the Late War. 1879

THE

NEW SOUTH

INVESTIGATED

BY
D. AUGUSTUS STRAKER

ARNO PRESS
A NEW YORK TIMES COMPANY
New York ☆ 1973

Reprint Edition 1973 by Arno Press Inc.

Reprinted from a copy in
The Columbia University Library

The American South
ISBN for complete set: 0-405-05058-5

Manufactured in the United States of America

———◆———

Library of Congress Cataloging in Publication Data

Straker, David Augustus, d. 1908.
　The new South investigated.

　　(The American South)
　　Reprint of the ed. published by Ferguson
Printing Co., Detroit.
　　1. Southern States.　2. Negroes--Southern
States.　I. Title.　II. Series.
F215.S89　1973b　　　301.45'19'6073075　　72-11348
ISBN 0-405-05064-X

THE
NEW SOUTH
INVESTIGATED

D Augustus Straker

THE

NEW SOUTH

INVESTIGATED.

BY

D. AUGUSTUS STRAKER,

Attorney at Law and Solicitor in Chancery
at the Detroit Bar, Michigan.

Author of " Reflections on the Life and Times of
Toussaint L'Overture."

DETROIT, MICH.
Ferguson Printing Company.
1888.

Copyright 1888,
By D. AUGUSTUS STRAKER.

PREFACE.

The publication of these views in book form is the result of many requests, verbal and written, by friends. Extracts of some of these requests I append, hoping that my readers will accept them as a sufficient and excusable reason for this attempt.

My experience in the South ranges through a period of more than a decade of years, and includes a residence in South Carolina, and various visits to other States, where I have delivered addresses and lectures on many occasions. During these years, extending from 1875 to 1887, various and vast changes have taken place in this portion of our country, sufficient to entitle said change to the title "New South." By this it is not intended to prove, as is sometimes erroneously alleged, that there is an entire transformation of the South from Old into New, so that there is no vestige of old customs, no trace of ancient laws or habits, no *indicia* of slavery or civil law, no old homesteads nor even family cast of countenance preserved. This is not the meaning of the "New South" as treated in the following pages, but it is intended only to portray the evident changes which have occurred since the emancipation of the slaves and the reconstruction of the States engaged in civil war. These events have always produced change where they have occurred, and strange it would be, indeed, if similar results did not occur in our land. Truly has someone said that the "Old South" means all those facts and forces that characterized the geographical South, particularly as moulded by the institution of slavery. It is a political designation. But even the most inveterate conservatives and strongest partizans North and South are compelled to recognize a change and to acknowledge that the South of 1886 is not the South of 1850, 1863, or even 1870. The "New South" marks the beginning and progress of great changes, sociological and industrial, and the following pages will thus treat the topic.

The march of civilization has been east, north and west, marked by all the social, political and industrial changes which history records. It must complete its work. It has commenced south, its first fruit being the destruction of slavery. Since then it has borne more and varied fruit, enjoyed and to be enjoyed by the youth of the present and of the future citizens of a new South. In order to fully understand the South, the "New South," if you please, one must place it side by side with the "Old South," see its change; see the negro as a slave and as a free man; as a chattel and as a recognized human being; as a nonentity in the government to which he owed allegiance, and as a citizen with the constitutional rights thereof, enjoyable if not enjoyed. See the negro changed from deep ignorance and superstition to a high degree of enlightment and religious culture; from a poor, homeless creature to a possessor of the soil and a taxpayer. See "King

Cotton" upon the pedestal of requited labor, however inadequate, and the mineral resources no longer lying dormant in the bowels of the earth, but brought to its surface by a new industry and laid at the feet of man, controlled by his power; see the vast change in architecture, the new style of houses occupying the places of the old-fashioned mansion—the habitation of the slave owner; see chapels and schoolhouses where the slave-block once stood; see the man and brother growing up in a closer relationship in spite of caste prejudice. Now all this does not mean that the South in its new growth is perfect and without error, as some construe the new South to mean. Not at all; the South is still old in many respects. Its customs, its habits, its ideas, its practices, are not entirely new; but they are not entirely old. I have lived and seen many changes in the South for the better during the time I have lived there, and I believe it is necessary to the proper understanding of the South and its people to view it from the standpoint of a new growth. The better understanding between the people of these two sections, is "a consummation devoutly to be wished."

It is not all it should be, even at the present time. It need learn the ways of the North and adopt the energy of the people of this section. Its education must be a new one to meet its new necessities and emergencies. There are enough inherent possibilities in the South to make it a great section of our country. This is seen not only in its material development since the late civil war, but in the development of new ideas. The inequality between the two races—the Anglo Saxon and Negro—resting upon the fallacious belief of the inherent inferiority of the latter and a divine law of the necessity to keep them separate, unequal in privileges and unrecognized in manhood, has begun to stir up the minds of some in the Old South, and to produce new ideas fitted for the new development. Judge Tourgee prepared the ground in his "Fool's Errand" and "Bricks Without Straw;" Mr. Geo. W. Cable and Dr. Atticus Haygood planted the first seed. Nay, even earlier than this, men lived in the South who, seeing the end and results of the war, regretted its commencement and adopted the new ideas necessary for reformation and progress. They were few and apart, but many knew of them.

In South Carolina, Senator Hampton, F. W. McMaster, Sr., and others, urged the necessity of educating the negro as a safeguard against corrupt government as well as a right belonging to them. These views have multiplied and men have increased in the same. In fact, admitting the inherent power of the South to grow into a new shape from the old, it must be admitted that it has had infused into it the spring of a new life from the North. Men and women of this region have given their money and their lives to save the South from becoming defunct as a government or a country. The education and development of the Negro is to be traced chiefly to this source; and the writer, as one of the Negro race, is indebted to this spirit of the North and its deeds for a portion of his education.

But the chief aim and purpose of these pages is to portray, even though imperfectly done, the South as it has grown in the past twenty-four years; and to bring closer the two sections. Nothing but kindness, allied with firmness, on the part of the North, and truth and justice in the South, can do this. Take nothing for granted against the South. Prove all things; hold fast to the truth. The great problem of the day, as is seen to be solved in the South, but not exclusively there, is the true relationship of the Negro with the Anglo Saxon. I shall devote a few pages hereafter to the growth and development of the negro race in the South, by giving brief sketches of the lives of some of the race who have become marked and shining pillars in the "New South," and without regarding whom, the "New South Discussed" is incomplete. The intellectual growth of this race chiefly is the marvel of the age, as is the disbelief of its capacity and fitness to rise alongside with the white brother—the wonder in human disbelief and perverseness. Nearly fifty-three millions of people in this country worship God falsely in their belief that the Negro is an inferior being and unfitted for their association and privileges. This idea must be reformed; but I will not discuss this topic in these pages but leave them to abler hands. I therefore introduce my book to the public, with the hope that "the *will* will be taken for the deed," and what I have not done attribute to my earnest desire to do for the benefit of a common people of a common country.

D. AUGUSTUS STRAKER,
AUTHOR.
DETROIT, Mich., August 1, 1888.

CONTENTS.

I.—GENERAL VIEW 17
II.—THE SOUTH POLITICALLY . . . 54
III.—THE NEW SOUTH POLITICALLY . . 69
IV.—THE SOCIAL PROBLEM OF THE SOUTH 77
V.—THE NEGRO AS A CITIZEN . . . 108
VI.—PROTECTION VERSUS FREE TRADE 134
VII.—THE NECESSITY FOR A BROADER AND HIGHER EDUCATION IN THE SOUTH 143
VIII.—CAPITAL AND LABOR; AND THE TRUE RELATION OF THE COLORED CITIZEN TO LABOR ORGANIZATIONS IN AMERICA 168
IX.—THE NEGRO—PAST, PRESENT AND FUTURE 201
X.—CONCLUSION 228

INTRODUCTION.

I herewith introduce the following letters and extracts received from distinguished citizens in various parts of the country, expressing their views briefly on the topic discussed in this work, and the benefit to be derived from the publication of the same. It will be seen from these letters how deeply interested the public mind is on this vital topic, so strongly interwoven with the future welfare of our whole country. These letters afford to the reader an opportunity to see how far the author's views agree with those of other citizens. In the following pages I have, in the language of ex-Governor Daniel H. Chamberlain of New York (late of South Carolina), endeavored as best I can to "exorcise the demon of party spirit" in my discussion of the "New South." It must, however, be admitted that the "demon" of the controlling party spirit of the South today, is not easily exorcised; it must, nevertheless, die under the influences of such a "New South" as it is to be hoped will ere long appear: a South of progressive ideas, enlarged industry, broad education and obedience to law and order.

EXTRACTS FROM LETTERS RECEIVED AS TO PUBLICATION OF THE WORK.

Your lecture, to which I had the pleasure of listening, was very instructive to me, and gave evidence of great liberality in

12   INTRODUCTION.

treatment. The subjects with which you deal are of great interest to us in the North. I need not say that in the development and prosperity of the colored citizens of the South, we owe you earnest sympathy. I believe you have found the key to the advancement of your race. I hope you will publish your views—I desire to read your book.
    Sincerely yours,
      GEO. FRED. WILLIAMS,
        Counsellor at Law,
        Boston, Mass.

I am glad to learn that you intend to publish your lecture, "The New South." It is a forcible presentation of our case.
    Very truly,
      GEO. L. RUFFIN,
        Boston, Mass.

I regard it as a masterly production. It is clear, comprehensive, impartial and reassuring. It seems to me that the American people would read with interest and profit a work from your pen in which you would present "The New South."
    Yours truly,
      T. McCANTS STUART,
        Attorney at Law,
        New York, N. Y.

"The New South," an excellent paper on the Negro problem, excellent alike for the soundness of its thought and the method of its treatment."—*The Detroit Plaindealer.*

The above were received from such persons who listened to my lecture, entitled "The New South," which is now enlarged to the size of a book, in which much more is said and my views enlarged upon. The following is concerning this book as now compiled: AUTHOR.

"You can scarcely do any better work than the publication of your book entitled "The New South Investigated." Your literary ability, your knowledge and experience and your downright earnestness, will enable you to do for the subject what few others would do. You have not only lived at the South, but you have lived at the heart of the South. * * The knowledge obtained from what you have seen, felt and heard in that quarter will be valuable. Very truly yours,
FRED'K DOUGLASS.
ANACOSTIA D. C., July, 1888.

DETROIT, MICH., July 16th, 1888.
D. A. STRAKER, Esq.,

DEAR SIR:—Replying to yours of the 14th inst., inviting an expression from me as to my views on "the propriety and benefit of publishing a book on 'the new South,'" I have only to say, that as yet, in my opinion, "the new South," as the North and all loyal citizens desire to see it, has but an ideal existence.

It is wealthy in its undeveloped resources, and attractive in its climate; peculiar in its reconstructed politics, but still far removed from its proper relations under the law and constitution to *all* the people of its own and those of the sister States.

The people of the North cannot fail to be interested in its advancement and prosperity; and under proper and safe conditions, they will be disposed to aid in the investment and loan of their capital for this end.

However, two things are essential before Northern capital will flow South, and Northern confidence in its protection there, will be accepted; and these are, first, a free delivery and an honest return of the people's ballots under the Constitution of the United States; and, second, the enactment, or at least the enforcement of such laws as will guarantee and protect personal property, personal liberty and personal security.

Southern men may say, that they already have these; but, as a matter of fact, we know the contrary to be the truth. These things being once conceded as truly and practically established, the North will be cordial and kind, and evince the same degree of reciprocity in traffic and intercourse, as now exists between them and the people of all other States not included within the political designation of "the South." Until then, the "New South," like Plato's republic, will exist only in idea—the romance of a dream.

If your book will in anywise tend, by the presentation of facts and arguments, to bring about this happy result, and so make our Union a harmonious one, one of our *entire* people (as our fathers intended, and the great majority of the Northern people desire it should be), I shall be glad to see it published and carefully read, and I would cheerfully give my name to its subscription roll.

Yours respectfully,

D. BETHUNE DUFFIELD,
DETROIT, MICH.

NEW YORK, July 5, 1888.

D. AUGUSTUS STRAKER, Esq.,
DETROIT, MICH.

DEAR SIR:—I am informed that you intend to prepare a book entitled "The New South Investigated;" and you indicate that your attention will be specially directed to the industrial and social aspects of the South at present. Such a work, if done in a fair and just spirit, with an eye bent upon the *new* South rather than the *old*, and written with a purpose to make the best of the present as well as to make the future hopeful, exorcising the demon of party spirit and political rancor, will do much good and is a work which may well excite the patriotic ambition of any intelligent man and especially a colored man. I sincerely hope you will do this work in the spirit above indicated, and you can rely, in that case, upon my applause and my assistance to any extent compatible with the very busy pursuit of my profession here. No one could have had better opportunities than you have had for studying these questions, and I believe you have sufficient intellectual and literary power to make such a book interesting and valuable.

Yours very truly,

D. H. CHAMBERLAIN.
NEW YORK, N. Y.

DETROIT, July 6, 1888.

I regard Prof. Straker's book, "The New South Investigated," as a timely contribution to the discussion of the most unique chapter of our political history. When the historian of the future notes how the Republican party increased the representation of the South by enfranchising the slaves and making them citizens, and how the increased representation was retained by the Democracy while the votes of the newly-made citizens were suppressed by fraud, he will wonder at the patience with which the outrage was endured.

COL. JOHN ATKINSON,
Att'y at Law.

Prof. Straker is a well-poised, cultured man; he is equipped with a pride and hope for his race; he believes in them, and his book, bristling with an armament of logic and of fact, will form an argument as well as an incentive to high endeavor and healthy growth of his race. I should trespass on the domain of true criticism did I say more than this. He is my friend and I love him; my peer in the law and I honor him; my brother in that bond that makes the brotherhood of man next only to the fatherhood of God.

The need of such a work is apparent. It seeks to acquaint the world with the past, present and future of the South; to develope its industrial and commercial interests; to show how in diversity of pursuits is to be found the highest prosperity of the South. The North knows little of the resources and the immense advantages it holds out to labor and capital, and how protection to her industries will eventuate in the breaking up of a solid South. The North needs this book; and its wide circulation will do much to bring to view the true status of the South.

COL. SYLVESTER LARNED.
DETROIT, MICH., July 6, 1888.

NEW YORK, July 10, 1888.

No people ever enjoyed civil liberty who had not the courage to fight for it and the intelligence to preserve it after they have got it. Our people have got to solve the Southern problem themselves. As long as they remain poor and cowardly, they will be robbed and defrauded of their rights.

THOS. FORTUNE.

INTRODUCTION.

SALISBURY, N. C., July 23d, 1888.
From the Rev. J. C. Price, D.D., President of Livingston College.
HON. D. A. STRAKER:

MY DEAR FRIEND—"The South is, indeed, "New" in some respects; but the 'New South" we hear of and read about so frequently is not new absolutely as many would have the world believe.

There is a "New South," and there is an "Old South." The evidences of the existence of both are not tangible. In other words it is the "New Old South." If the "New South" is all it purports to be, it can bear investigation; but on the other hand, if it is not what the name implies, it ought to be willing to "stand convicted." Out of your large experience and very superior culture the country will not look in vain for a very interesting, instructive and timely book in "The New South Investigated."

All who know something of your ability feel that the interests of the South and the nation will be safe in your hands. *You know the South.*

THE NEW SOUTH.

CHAPTER I.

GENERAL VIEW.

There is no portion of our common country which is possessed of more interest to the true patriot than that known as the South. In the early times of the republic it bore a noble part in the struggle for independence and national existence, and the pages of history are illumined with the brave deeds of its sons, the eloquence of its orators and the wisdom of its statesmen. It also has been the theatre of human slavery, and within its confines, for more than two hundred years, have lived a race of people who were held in cruel bondage by their fellow man. To sustain the institution of slavery, and the principles upon which it was founded, it has witnessed and endured the awful carnage of thousands of its citizens upon the battlefield. To maintain the principle that slavery was both legal and right, a principle which although false was by the South sacredly believed to be right, it engaged in the most horrible internecine strife known to the annals of history. The devastations of civil war have marked the South indelibly in all its ramifications. From the citadel of wealth it has descended to the plane of comparative poverty. The industry of its past has been changed; its citizens are changed; its education has been changed, and during the past twenty-five years it has had a transitional period from "Old South" into "New South." The phrase "New South," indicates a previous condition from the now existing one. A brief retrospect of the condition of the South in the past, and a survey of it today, will doubtless enable the reader to comprehend its possibilities, ascertain its progress, and fully appreciate the hopes entertained for its future. Men have written what is called the history of the United States; but the true history of our country, comprising North, East, West and South, and showing even the average development of the American citizen, is yet to be written. And this cannot be until *all* of its citizens enjoy the fullest opportunity for intellectual, industrial and moral advancement in the North, East, West and South alike; and all sections of our common country are in perfect harmony and intent in producing this development.

Before the civil war, in which the two sections of our country engaged in deadly strife, the South presented to the civilized world a government whose corner-stone was slavery. This system divided its people into two classes of several subdivisions—bond and free—which comprised the rich and the poor, the educated and the ignorant, black and white. This kind of social government, in its aristocratic form and practice, kept in effect the poor whites of the South in a state of serfdom, and the Negro in a state of total subjection and ignorance. In short, it was the lord and the peasant, with the slave added. In this condition, self-development was impracticable, save in muscle, as labor enriched the slave-owner, and kept poor and ignorant poor white and slave alike. The social relationship was protected by barriers of pedigree, and every avenue for advancement in such knowledge as would enlighten the human mind, was securely closed by law. The schoolhouse was for the rich only. All this was necessary, in order to maintain the bondage of the Negro and the peasantry of the poor whites. But meanwhile this condition prevailed, the entire South was in a state of stagnation. It moved forever in the groove which such men as Clay and Calhoun would mark out for it. This was seen in its industrial progress. Commerce was confined to one production only. "Cotton was King." Lands were held like unto the feudal times. Alienation of real property was little known. Hundreds and thousands of acres were the possession of one man, or one family, and descended from one generation to another, and was parcelled out to tenants. The article, so called, of commerce most pursued was human flesh, which was bought and sold as a commodity. Industry, in its broadest sense, was almost unknown. The arts and sciences were not cultivated, and invention, "the mother of necessity," had no mother or father in the South, and was, therefore, *nullus filius*—nobody's child.

This, briefly, was the condition which marked the South in the past. It was not a condition to promote the highest welfare of this section of our country; it was, moreover, at variance in its progress with the other portions of the country, and in nowise received that healthful influence of inter-commerce, or con-association in any of the methods of progress. And why? Because of that political mysticism known as "State Sovereignty," which meant the independence of the several States from the Federal Government in all respects, except as the States consented to be governed, and as they themselves construed such consent. This idea kept the Southern States from the benefit of the industrial influence of the sister States of the North, and this estrangement following was fostered by its statesmen, who translated true patriotism to mean sectional superiority. This condition, and this doctrine, grew and bore fruit—the Civil War. The devastations of this strife are yet to be seen in many parts of the South today. The fearful loss of lives, and waste of treasure, are within the memory of many. By the blight of this war, men and women were made poor in the South, who were formerly rich; industry was swept away, lands were laid waste, education had departed, government was chaotic, men were desperate, women were mournful; but a *race* was emancipated, a sufficient reason for all else. And that fearful condition of the South might have lasted until today, but for the magnanimity of that noble patriot, that grand hero and soldier, whom we have laid in the chamber of eternal rest, General Ulysses S. Grant, who by bravery, courage and unbending purpose defeated the enemy of the Union of our great country, and thus forever buried the false idea of independent States to the Union, with its falser help-meet—slavery. But upon the grave of this error was planted the new South, by General Grant giving to General Lee his parole at Appomatox, and bidding him tell his soldiers to take their horses and return to their homes, to the *peaceful pursuit of agriculture*. By this magnanimous act of good feeling and statesmanship, followed by his patriotic utterance a few years after: "Let us have peace," the noble hero, soldier and saviour of his country, inspired his fellow citizens of the South with the hope of reviving it. It is a happy thought to know, and a happier one to perceive, that although "war may stride over a land with the crushing step of a giant, unpeopling here a village, and there a city, until every dwelling is a sepulchre, the sky itself brazen, and the beautiful greenness gives place to a parched desert, a wide waste of unproductive desolation," that yet these are only physical evils, and that "the wild flower will bloom again in peace, where the battlefield was, and that above the crushed skeleton the destroying angel will retire and the nation will again breathe freely." So it has been with the South, to a very great extent, and I believe that this revival had its source in the feeling created by General Grant on the battlefield, which was, that despite the civil strife which had just closed, the North and South still remained brethren, and citizens of a common country. This sentiment carried into practice placed the dead hero of Vicksburg higher on the roll of great warriors than has yet been attained, before or since, by earth's bravest soldier. Cæsar conquered nations by his large armies, and never ceased to seek to conquer until insatiate ambition caused his ruin. Alexander the Great, after conquering well nigh the known world, yet sighed for further power and dominion without regard to the benefit his conquests gave to mankind. Napoleon and Frederic the Great loved war for the power it gave them. Wellington, it is said, only fought for a peerage. Not so with him who lies at Riverside Park, N.Y. In him patriotism, such as the world had not seen since the days of the black warrior, Toussaint L'Overture, marked his every action, both as soldier and statesman. Toussaint L'Overture and General Grant as soldiers, showed their greatness by their magnanimity towards the foe. It will be remembered, that when Toussaint L'Overture had conquered the armies of the French proconsul, Napoleon sought through General Maitland to make terms of peace with the Haytien chief, and some one of Toussaint's generals, learning of Maitland's intended visit, sought to induce Toussaint L'Overture to seize and keep the French General as an hostage against the enemy; but it will also be remembered how the noble hearted Negro Chief of the Haytien Army rebuked his tempter saying, "tell General Maitland my word is my honor;" and to his tempter said: "Sir, I am incapable of baseness." Having received General Maitland, Toussaint requested him to tell Napoleon Bonaparte that he sought not honor, fame nor riches; but only liberty for his people from a cruel bondage, and justice and equality for them before the law. In this manly, brave, christian, statesmanlike and patriotic conduct, Toussaint furnished a lesson in the history of true civilization in warfare, which General Grant did not think unworthy of following in his course towards General Lee, as was seen both at Appomatox and afterwards in Washington, when Secretary Stanton sought to nullify his words of promise to the conquered chief. Truly did the poet Blair describe these two great soldiers, when he wrote: "that the greatest man on earth can no sooner commit an injury, than a good man can make himself greater by forgiving it." Both of these warriors distinguished themselves by being fearless in duty, yet full of affection for their brethren, self-denying, zealous for the public good, magnanimous without being proud, humble without being mean, just without being harsh, manly in feeling, reliable in their word, they both have died a bright example to the soldier, the statesman and the ruler. The life and character of these two greatest of warriors and patriots are the noblest monuments of their country, and the pride and affection of a once down-trodden race of two countries. Toussaint L'Overture gave liberty to the Haytien slave; General Grant to the American bondsman.

Now let us revert to the condition of the South at the close of the war. The first step in placing the South in its proper place under a new condition, was the measure of reconstruction enacted by Congress, whereby as Senator Sumner expressed it, the Southern States became *tabula rasa*, clean slates, and the enactment of the 13th, 14th and 15th Amendments to the Constitution, gave to the ex-slave citizenship and suffrage. The next step of importance was the education of the masses. The Negro needed education to fit him for his new responsibilities of citizen and voter; the poor whites needed education to fit them for the new condition of the South, which for the first time had presented an opportunity for all alike to rise in the scale of human progress. But this movement towards the education of the Negro, found great opposition from the native whites, who, lacerated in feeling and debased in pride, saw in the education of the Negro the total oblivion of the former rule of an aristocratic class. Blind to their best interests, they burnt school houses, and persecuted Northern teachers. But it is also true, that political demagogues, under the guise of teaching Republican doctrine, fomented strife between the two races in the South at that period, and used the Negro as a political tool to further their own end and aim, which was chiefly political fortune. This was pulling at both ends, which invariably produces no advancement. It gave the seed of education no opportunity to grow. And this is no apology for Copiah, Danville or Hamburg; but is a fair statement of the true condition of the then South. It soon became evident that while the newly emancipated race needed intellectual advancement, the defeated Southerner needed moral elevation—one from the plane of ignorance and superstition to the elevation of knowledge and morality; the other from gross social and political darkness, to the knowledge of the light of a new civilization, a new condition, which should cause both races in the South to feel a common interest in a common welfare. In this changed condition, stagnation marked the South; lands were unoccupied, industry was lifeless; capital shunned the South. The chief stock in trade was, among the Democrats, the formation of Rifle Clubs and Ku Klux Klans. While this condition lasted the South stood still; yet there was a leaven leavening silently and unseen the whole South. It was education, moral elevation and industry, taught by the believers in freedom and equality for all. The South received an education from the North other than that taught in the school house. It received new constitutions and new methods of industry and development; but while it received these benefits, mal-administration prevailed in public affairs by the party in power to an indescribable extent, which led in 1876 to a political revolution—nay, worse, a usurpation of government. The remedy, it will be seen, was worse than the disease. This revolution arose from two causes. On the one hand the Republican leaders in the South sought only political fortune through office, and disregarded the true development of the South. On the other hand the Democrats sought reformation by violence too horrible to mention. The spirit of usurpation took the place of needed reformation, which is now sought to be justified by the assertion that the end justified the means. The Republican leaders of the white race in the South tried to serve God and mammon. They worshipped at the shrine of social distinction, at the same time they proclaimed equality before the law for the Negro. Indeed the whole Republican party, which had made the Negro a citizen and voter, failed to protect him in the exercise of his suffrage in this crisis. In this it showed its weakness. This weakness of the Republican party in 1876, was the Democratic party's opportunity which it seized and put to purpose in its own behalf. Democratic power in the South is but the result of Republican timidity to enforce the law.

But let us deal with the South more from an industrial than a political standpoint at present, as we shall return to this topic later on. The South today has, amid all its troubles, political and otherwise, made great advancement in industry, education and commerce. Our land owners are now ready and willing to utilize their lands and not let them lie uncultivated. Our farmers no longer confine themselves to the growing of cotton only, but are engaged in the more varied industry of planting corn and rice. This latter article is cultivated in South Carolina to a degree of almost perfection, as all those who visited the late Cotton Exposition, held at New Orleans, can testify, if they saw it. Manufactories begin to dot the South in all of its principal cities and towns. Who that has visited the cities of Augusta, Atlanta, Savannah and Macon, in Georgia; Charleston, Greenville and Columbia, in South Carolina; Selena, Montgomery, Birmingham and Anniston, in Alabama; the City of New Orleans; Jacksonville, in Florida; and other cities of the South, can fail to discover the great advancement in the industry of the South in the past twenty years. The hum of the spinning wheel, and the noise of the manufactories' whistles are now heard in every principal city in the South today, and the ring of the anvil follows the church bell. The spirit of industry has taken hold of our water-power and our mineral resources, and has utilized them as far as the capital of the South will admit. Along our canals are being built numerous factories, and the cotton which we now grow is no longer entirely sent to foreign parts for manufacture, but is manufactured on the spot at Graniteville, Greenville, Columbia, Charleston, Atlanta, Savannah and Augusta. This shows the need for a protective tariff for the South. From the bowels of the earth we now dig iron, coal, gold and other minerals. Our industries are more varied than is generally known. We not only manufacture cotton, but we turn the cotton seed into oil. We have successfully cultivated the tea plant. The tea farm is now reckoned among the industrial pursuits of South Carolina. Our mills are numerous. We have the paper-mill, the saw-mill, the grist-mill, moulding our future alongside of other industries. Our railroads also show the advancement of the South. The old iron rail is now supplanted by the modern steel rail, and the dog-kennel depot is supplanted in many places by the beautiful artistic building of modern days. We have the improved air-brake; we run with greater speed. I remember when, not more than ten years ago, it took twelve hours from Charleston to Columbia, a distance of 130 miles. To-day it is reached by rail in five hours. We even *kill* more people on the railroad than we did before, and then, following in the march of progressive ideas, we have our railroad attorneys to plead as a defense, "contributory negligence or common hazard." To illustrate this great advancement in industry, which characterizes the "New South," I will show in detail the advancement of the several industries I have generally mentioned as reported in South Carolina.

First, the resources which are capable of development in the State, and to which capital and skilled labor are invited, are 17,000,000 acres of land, of which only 4,000,000 are now in cultivation. These lands, such as are good, can be bought from $2 to $10 per acre. The special agent of the census on forestry estimates that there is now standing in the State 6,000,000 feet of pine lumber. Gold and silver are to be found in nearly all of the upper counties, and at present only twelve mines are being worked, and none of them have been developed to their full capacity. The water-power of the State is estimated at 3,000,000 horse-power, and only 15,000 horse-power is being used by all of the manufacturing establishments.

Now, as to advancement. In agriculture, corn has increased in twelve years 9,431,528 bushels, or 124 per cent. Oats, 7,316,377 bushels, or twelve fold the yield in 1870. Wheat, 1,150,360 bushels, or 170 per cent. Rice, 32,379,754 pounds, or 100 per cent. Cane syrup, 193,580 gallons, or 31 per cent. Sweet potatoes, 2,502,714 bushels, or 136 per cent. Irish potatoes, 303,938 bushels, or 365 per cent., and cotton has been increased 396,470 bales, or 176 per cent. The increase in manufactures has also been marvelous. The value of the total product of cotton mills in 1860 was $713,050; in 1880, $2,895,769; in 1883, $7,963,198, an increase in three years as you perceive of 175 per cent., and proof conclusive that free labor is more conducive to the prosperity of a people than slave labor. The South Carolina phosphates, which were discovered in 1867 at a place called Lambs, about twelve miles from Charleston, on the Ashley river, and which were declared valuable by the eminent scientist, Dr. St. Julien Ravenel, have increased from 20,000 tons in 1870, to 409,000 tons in 1886. There are at present fourteen land and eleven river mining companies, and they have an aggregate capital of $2,505,000, and employ 1,935 hands, and pay out $622,860 in wages. The value of their products amount to $2,190,000.

Upon a royalty of $1.00 per ton, $1,279,170 has been paid into the State Treasury.

Now, as to our railroads. From the small railroad commenced in 1827 in South Carolina, which was the first effort in America to build a railroad for locomotive power, has sprung and increased to the magnificent railroad system of the present day, which embraces the South Carolina Railway Company, the Columbia, Greenville, Charlotte and Augusta, the Charleston and Savannah, the Port Royal, the Augusta and Knoxville, the Greenwood, Laurens and Spartanburg, the Wilmington and Columbia, the Greenville and Laurens, the Cheraw and Chester, and the Chester and Lenoir. The total assessed value of all railroad property in this State on the 1st January, 1884, was $15,263,366. The aggregate mileage 1,495. This is but the proof of the advancement of one of the Southern States. It is reasonable to suppose that the others are proportionate, and that the South today may, with justice, in a large degree, be called *the "New South"* industrially.

The following statistics, taken from publications in reliable news-journals will, when read, sustain my views of a new South, industrially:

MAGIC GROWTH OF THE SOUTH.—THE INDUSTRIAL PROGRESS OF THE LAST THREE MONTHS.—IMMENSE AND ALMOST INCREDIBLE DEVELOPMENT OF THE IRON AND COAL INTEREST.—STEADY PROGRESS IN COTTON MILLS, MINING AND QUARRYING AND A HUNDRED OTHER KINDS OF ENTERPRISES.

BALTIMORE, October 14.—The Baltimore *Manufacturers' Record*, in its quarterly review of the South's industrial growth, to be published tomorrow, says:

"Even the West, in the days of its greatest progress, probably never saw such tremendous strides of progress as some portions of the South are now making. The centre of interest for some time has been in the iron and steel industries, and in these the activity has been wonderful, although in other lines of diversified manufactures there is also remarkable progress.

"Among the principle iron and steel enterprises now under way, are five new furnaces, Basic Steel Works, and 1,400 coke ovens, by the Tennessee Coal, Iron and Railroad Company, who have already five furnaces in operation. This company has a capital of $10,000,000, and when the new furnaces are completed will have a daily capacity of about 1,400 tons of pig iron. Two furnaces are now building for the Debardeleben Coal and Iron Company; one by Samuel Thomas and associates, of Pennsylvania; two under contract at Sheffield, Ala.; two by Nashville and New York capitalists, at South Pittsburg, Tenn.; one by the Coalburg Coal and Coke Company, of Birmingham; one at Ashland, Ky.; one at Ætna, Tenn.; one at Calera, Ala.; an $800,000 iron company at Florence, Ala.; Bessemer Steel Works at Chattanooga, Tenn., and Richmond, Va., two stone works, each with a capital of $200,000, at Birmingham, Ala.; two iron pipe works, one to be the largest in the United States, at Chattanooga, and a similar enterprise at Wheeling, Ala.; a $600,000 company has been organized to build an iron manufacturing town at Bessemer, Ala.; a $3,000,000 company, composed of Northern and Southern capitalists, has purchased a large part of South Pittsburg, where two furnaces are in operation and where three more are to be built, and also iron pipe works and other manufacturing enterprises, while two other iron centers are to be developed near Birmingham, one by the North Birmingham Land Company, and the other by the Tennessee Coal, Iron and Railroad Company.

"During the last nine months there have been organized in the South forty-two ice factories, fifty-six foundries and machine shops, many of them of large size, one Bessemer steel rail mill, sixteen miscellaneous iron works, including iron pipe works, bridge and bolt works, etc., five stove foundries, nineteen gas works, twenty-three electric light companies, eight agricultural implement factories, 114 mining and quarrying enterprises, twelve carriage and wagon factories, nine cotton mills, nineteen furniture factories, twenty-one water works, forty-four tobacco factories, seventy-one flour mills, 362 lumber mills (not counting small portable saw mills), including saw and planing mills, sash and door factories, stave, handle, shingle, hub and spoke, shuttle-block factories, etc., in addition to which there was a large number of miscellaneous enterprises."

The *Manufacturers' Record* says further, that during the first nine months of 1886 the amount of capital, including the capital stock of incorporated companies, represented by new manufacturing and mining enterprises organized or chartered at the South, and in the enlargement of old plants and rebuilding of mills that were destroyed by fire, aggregates $83,814,200, against $52,386,300 for the corresponding period of 1885.

INDUSTRIAL PROGRESS AT THE SOUTH.

BALTIMORE, January 28.—The Baltimore *Manufacturers' Record*, published yesterday its annual review of the industrial growth of the South and the progress made in the development of the manufacturing and mining interests of that section during 1885, notwithstanding the general depression in business throughout the country. A noticeable feature is the wide diversity of new enterprises, which include almost every industry in the country. The amount of capital, including capital stock of incorporated companies organized during the year, and that used in enlarging and rebuilding structures destroyed by fire, aggregates $66,812,000, divided among the fourteen Southern States as follows: Alabama, $7,841,000; Arkansas, $1,220,000; Florida, $2,019,000; Georgia, $2,500,000; Kentucky, $18,304,200; Louisiana, $2,118,500; Maryland, $6,668,800; Mississippi, $761,500; North Carolina, $3,230,000, South Carolina, $856,000; Tennessee, $2,692,000; Texas, $3,232,000; Virginia, $3,314,000; West Virginia, $12,056,000; total, $66,812,000. Summing up some statistics of the South's progress since 1880, the *Record* shows that since then 10,400 miles have been added to the railroad mileage of the section, the building of which, added to the investments in old roads and their improvement, foots up $571,000,000; the actual cost of the railroads of the South and their equipment according to statistics, being over $1,250,000,000, against $679,800,000 in 1880. The assessed value of property in the South has increased nearly $1,000,000,000 since 1879.

THE GROWING SOUTH.

The rapid and remarkable growth of the South has now become one of the commonplaces of American political economy. We find in the *Times-Democrat* some figures, which show the increase in the valuation of the Southern States in the last nine years. Here is the table from the Assessors' returns.

	1886-'87		1879-'80	
STATES.	Assessment.	Rate of Taxation.	Assessment.	Rate of Taxation.
Alabama	$ 172,528,933	6¼	$ 117,486,181	7
Arkansas	140,531,033	4	86,409,364	6½
Florida	76,611,409	4	29,471,618	7
Georgia	306,507,578	3½	235,650,530	5
Kentucky	483,491,690	5¼	318,037,875	4 3-5
Louisiana	219,000,000	6	158,587,495	11
Mississippi	125,000,000	2¼	106,594,708	3¼
N. Carolina	202,752,622	3¼	156,100,202	3¼
S. Carolina	151,495,056	5¼	132,037,986	6.31
Tennessee	224,909,179	4	211,768,538	2
Texas	621,011,989	7¼	304,193,163	5
Virginia	340,760,960	4	308,455,135	6
Total	$3,064,800,443	4 3-5	$2,164,792,795	5 3-5

Florida has gained proportionately more than any other of the Southern States—nearly 200 per cent. since 1879. Texas shows a gain of more than 100 per cent., and an average gain in valuation of more than $35,000,000 a year. Alabama, Arkansas, Georgia, Kentucky, Louisiana and North Carolina, show smaller but still enormous gains. Virginia, Tennessee, South Carolina and Mississippi, have not been so fortunate as the rest of the South, yet they show a handsome increase. Doubtless the debt question in Virginia and Tennessee, and the uncertainty of labor in Mississippi and South Carolina, have somewhat retarded the growth of those States.

It should be noted that the increase in the rate of taxation in Kentucky, North Carolina, Tennessee and Texas, is mainly or solely due to increased appropriations for public schools.

In relation to this industrial advancement in the South, we may with profit turn our attention to the progress of the colored race therein. It is undeniable that in spite of oppression by laws and in social treatment, the colored citizen of the South has made incomparable progress. They have acquired property, real and personal, in sums of value astonishing to those who claim that they are incapable of thrift or industry. In Georgia the colored citizens pay taxes on upwards of seven million dollars worth of property. In Louisiana more than this; and in all of the Southern States they show by taxes an increase in the property they now possess. They are not so markedly advanced in industrial pursuits, such as manufactures, because the doors of technical industry are closed against them to a large extent on account of color. But this is not so strongly exercised against the colored man of the South at the present time, as heretofore. In the South, there are the colored mechanic, such as the carpenter, bricklayer, painter, tailor, shoemaker, blacksmith, wheelwright, cabinet maker and other artizans, who are employed as workmen of their trade. Indeed, in many places colored men are to be found as architects and contractors for work. The former spirit of prejudice exercised against the colored mechanic working alongside of the white, is more rapidly dying out in the South than it appears in the North. So great is the present spirit of industry in the South, that some States overstep themselves and enter upon cruelty in availing themselves of labor. This is done in South Carolina and Georgia. In the former State the shoe, cotton and hosiery factories are within the confines of the penitentiary, but South Carolina, like Georgia, is also engaged in hiring out by lease the convicts to persons for profit. This practice is not in the line of progress in the South, I must confess, and is to be condemned. By this system the convicts are leased out to contractors whose chief aim is to render his investment as profitable as he can, without regard to the life or health of the laborer, as a convict. His contract involves no interest whatever in the convict. If he die, he must be replaced; hence the treatment which the convicts often receive, at the hands of the contractor, or some brutal overseer, consists in chaining the convicts with heavy chains closely fitting their ankles, and in many cases the iron fetter eats into the bone of the feet, and amputation of the limb becomes necessary. The bed of the convict is often no more than straw, scattered as for a pig. His sleeping apartment is the stockade, which is but another name for a pig sty. It is seldom floored. His diet is of the lowest order, such as induces scurvy and its kindred diseases, and for discipline, his overseer is permitted to whip him, which is frequently so brutally done as to cause death. But cruel and despicable as all this is, it does not go without reproof. In South Carolina the press and the official authorities have been diligent in rebuking and arresting this uncivilized conduct; and yearly the legislature seeks to throw around the hired convict more and more protection. But the only true remedy is to abolish the cruel system altogether, and to provide for the labor of the convict within the prison walls. It is murder to hire a convict and permit him to be beaten or starved to death. The best safeguard against this cruel treatment, while the system exists, is to hang the cowardly wretch who would beat a man in chains to death. This system is the worst phase of capital against labor.

In regard to the opportunity denied the colored citizen to fully engage in the industrial pursuits, I will endeavor to show the inconsistency of the reason given for the practice exercised both in the North and the South; for this injustice is as much directed against the colored man of the North as of the South. In the South, while the colored citizen is denied admission into the manufactories, the reason given is, first, he is incapable of learning skilled labor; next, it brings him into social contact with his white brethren, yet the South utilizes this labor of the Negro convict in the penitentiary in a skilled form in making shoes, in carpentry, hosiery, tailoring and the like. In the North, the *idea* is against the equality of the Negro as a race; for he who will aid and assist the Negro to become educated as an individual in school, college or university, will close the doors of the workshop, the store of merchandise, the counting house and the printing press against him; and union leagues of trades deny him admission. Why is this? Is it because the mind of the American white citizen North and South is not yet fully educated to the principle of the "universal brotherhood of man and fatherhood of God?" In both North and South such practices belie the boasted civilization of our Anglo Saxon brethren. In the South especially it retards its advancement. What is the cruel purpose in educating the Negro in your schools of the North and then compelling him to work as a menial, or in the admitted groove of school teacher, preacher, hotel waiter or barber only? Or what benefit is it in the South to deny the privilege to the Negro of voluntarily becoming skilled in labor, where skilled labor is so much needed in developing its industries, while it is accepted in the form of convict labor? And all this distinction on account of his color. Is not this "cutting off the nose to spite the face?" I verily believe time will heal all of this, since the Negro is advancing in industry in the South in spite of all such obstacles. Let me illustrate. During the recent Cotton Exposition held at New Orleans, I forwarded a pair of pantaloons made by a colored person in Greenwood, S. C., who raised the sheep, sheared the wool, carded it, spun it, wove it into cloth, and made the pantaloons. This, to my mind, not only shows a spirit of industry, but capacity for it. The history of these pantaloons so interested the Superintendent of the Smithsonian exhibits at the Exposition, as to cause him to apply for them to be exhibited in the Institute in the City of Washington, D. C. This was granted, and they are doubtless there today. Another instance of the Negro's capacity for skilled and inventive labor, was seen in the marvelous exhibit of a complete locomotive made by a colored man of Kansas, and exhibited at the Exposition in New Orleans, and he, too, not an educated Negro. In South Carolina, the bronze palmetto tree, now situate on the grounds of the State House yard, was executed by a Negro as far back as the dark days of slavery; so, likewise, was Fort Sumter erected by a Negro under the superintendency of a white architect, who instituted the plan. How far the Negro was capable to learn the skilled arts of industry was fairly tested, even when the relationship of master and slave existed; hence today our colored mechanics in the South are skilled in the several trades, and the exclusion of the race to a fuller enjoyment of those privileges which they once received as slaves, and now ask to continue as freemen, shows plainly that the denial of the privilege is based on social condition and color, and not capacity. A fuller account of Negro progress in the South will be hereafter given.

The South has assumed a new role even in its fond pursuit of agriculture, not only as shown by statistics, showing an increased produce of articles, but also in its habits. Today in the South may be seen well nigh all of the most modern machinery used in farming. The science of agriculture is taught in our colleges and universities, so that the old idea that he who labored in the field was an inferior citizen to him who labored with the pen is now an exploded idea, and not infrequently do we take a modern

"Cincinnatus," and make him one of the rulers of the people. From all this is to be seen, that the South, in its new aspect of industry, needs only *capital* as the chief means of its development. It offers the fullest opportunity for this investment. Well nigh every industry of the North may be successfully carried on in the South. It is the future spot to which our overcrowded population of the North *must* bend its way. It has more unoccupied lands than any other section of the United States. Its forests of woods, its mineral resources, and its water power, only await capital and that industry which has given to America such cities as New York, Boston, Philadelphia, Chicago, Detroit and Baltimore, in which not only commerce holds sway, but in which beauty in architecture, and the growth of science, art, literature, and the spread of education are to be found. The immigration which the South needs is *not* European surplus labor, as I have shown that labor is full and efficient in this section for such purposes. What it needs is the skilled artizan, mechanic and other laborer of the North, and above all it needs Northern *push*, such as enables that section to build a railroad before a court can sign an injunction restraining it. Nothing will more effectively mould North and South into a homogeneous state than the introduction of like industries, and a common interest which money always produces, cemented by that feeling prevailing between the sections, and that good will, which General Grant in his last days so earnestly desired should take place, added to which there must be an obedience to law and order There are many who desire that this harmonious condition should exist and wonder at its delay. I venture the reason why it is so. It is because reform and progress are inseparable in their effects. It knows no classes, no condition, no color. To be effective those who seek advancement and full harmony and progress in the South, must in the spirit of the Good Master, go out into the highway and bring in the Negro as well as the white man of the South to the feast of reconciliation and good feeling. In other words, we must not be left in the bloody chasm while others shake hands over the chasm, since there will always be discord and discontent below. We alone did not dig the chasm, and ought not to be left unthought of in bridging it. There is room for all in the advancement of the South. Hands are ready, hearts are willing, and resources are large and numerous.

In South Carolina, a native white gentleman recently offered to purchase $25,000 worth of stock of the Saluda Factory on the banks of the Congaree River, on the Lexington side, and re-open the factory lately burnt, if he could find some Northern or other capitalist who would buy the remainder of the stock ($25,000 worth); and said that he would guarantee a good profit on the investment. This was a cotton factory, formerly operated with white and colored labor. "It will be again so operated," said the owner. He wants colored men to take stock, and he truly says, in speaking to the writer, "your race will never be fully respected until they represent such interests in common with the white race." He repudiates the idea that Negro labor is inferior to the labor of the white man under equal opportunity, and says he formerly operated both classes side by side in his factory, in menial as well as skilled labor. He said the white hands at first refused to work; but he gave them their choice to work or quit, and a majority remained. May not many of our Northern brethren profit by this lesson and manly course?

But I am told Northern capitalists will not come South to be socially bull-dozed. It is to be regretted that this charge is largely true whenever politics enter the question, but not otherwise. In the past every Northern capitalist coming South soon got into politics, which produced hostility and sectional strife; but gradually Northern capitalists have so benefited the South, as to call forth more liberality in exercise of their political rights while upbuilding this section, and calls into play self-preservation, expediency, policy and good sense, all of which teach the South to welcome capital without questioning its politics, and to give to every Northerner the right to be Republican or Democrat, as he chooses.

But the "New South" is not seen from an industrial standpoint only, but also from an educational view, and from a social and political aspect, each of which I shall now only briefly refer to but more fully treat hereafter. The "Old South," as I have already mentioned, sought only the education of the rich few. The masses were uneducated. The poor whites were taxed to educate the rich. The education to be attained in colleges or universities was not within the grasp of the poor white or the Negro. The Negro was kept in ignorance, that he may be the easier controlled, because the master well knew that knowledge was power. This damming up of knowledge and closing of all avenues of moral elevation produced gross ignorance among the poor whites and blacks, and caused the moral degradation of both in the South. But the civil war put an end to aristocratic government in the South, and opened the doors to those seeking education, without regard to race, color or previous condition. In this work of education Northern teachers were foremost, even though school houses were burnt and personal injuries often inflicted. Most of these wrongs were perpetrated out of a spirit to keep the Negro in ignorance on the one hand, and to indulge in revengeful hate on the other. But it must be admitted that there were some from the North who entered the South for profit to themselves only. Their aim was office and its emoluments, utterly disregarding the nature of the trust. Their conduct provoked much of the feeling which was manifested by the Southern whites towards the Negro. But, notwithstanding this, it cannot be denied that the South has benefited under the influence of Northern methods of industry and education. It had been a waste and a desert today but for such influences.

School houses have been built, likewise colleges and universities established. The South was both poor and unwilling to do this work of education. Now let us consider its present inclination. In South Carolina the State Superintendent recently reported that during the fiscal year 1883-4 the number of schools kept open was 3,452, and for 1884-5 there were 3,562, an increase of 80 schools. The number of teachers for 1883-4 was, white, 2,291, colored, 1,393; total, 3,684. For the year 1884-5 there were 2,342 white teachers, 1,431 colored; total, 3,773. The enrollment of pupils for 1883-4 was, white, 84,028, colored, 101,591; total, 185,619, and for 1884-5, white, 78,458, colored, 99,565. But here is the saddest feature. He says: "In 1883-4 the average length of the school session was four months. In 1884-5 it was only three and a half months." This is accounted for by the taxes of the State being a year behind. But I say this does not alter the effect. It shows that the South needs more education for the masses, and money to carry it on, for what is true of South Carolina is true of well nigh all the Southern states, and this too despite the private institutions of learning supported by the bounty of Northern friends and religious denominations. The chief need of the South today is higher education for the masses, which should be enjoyed by all alike. It is said in the South, especially, that the Negro is not fitted in capacity to receive the education of the higher branches. Is this true or is it an excuse for color prejudice? What is the evidence in the North, where his opportunity is unrestrained? Has he not shown himself in Harvard, Yale, Princeton and Ann Arbor as having like capacity and showing equal fitness with his white brother? The South needs to learn and is rapidly perceiving that the highest education of the new citizen is essential to its progress, nay its safety. The white citizen of the "New South" has awakened to this truth to a large extent, and today—I speak for South Carolina—many white citizens take a deep interest in the education of the masses, and are ready and willing to be taxed in their property for so great a good.

In South Carolina to-day, the ex-slave owner may be found in the common school, the college and the university teaching the Negro. In 1876, despite the great political upheaval, the people voted an amendment to the constitution, which requires the annual levy of two mills on the taxable property of the State for the support of the free public schools. A poll tax is collected from every male person between the ages of 21 and 60, and is applied to the support of the common schools. But, notwithstanding all this, the South does stand in need of assistance to carry on the great work of educating the masses. Of late a commendable spirit is shown in this direction. Indeed, finding by experience that the Negro in the South, as in all America, is here to stay, the Democratic party of the South has shown new zeal in his education, and in South Carolina, it must be admitted, that under Democratic rule the educational system has greatly advanced. In public meetings may be heard and seen the former slave owner and the abolitionist from Massachusetts, pleading together for the education of the citizen, black and white.

But the South is unable to provide adequately for the education of its great masses. In South Carolina the taxes produce a revenue of $400,000 annually. This in some counties is supplemented by special tax and contributions as well as the many private contributions of Northern friends and societies which support and maintain private institutions of learning. Yet it is seen that other than the schools in cities, the government is unable to maintain the schools longer than three or four months in each year. The national government is in duty bound to supply this need, because we are citizens of the United Stated as well as the several States in which we live, and it is the duty of the federal government to secure the blessings of liberty to all of its citizens, to promote the general welfare, and insure domestic tranquility by educating its citizens as the best method of doing so. But the States themselves are not relieved from their separate responsibility as States. The South owes the Negro education as a just debt, with interest accruing for two hundred and fifty years, and there are many who acknowledge this debt, and show their willingness to pay their part; others are not, and there are those who oppose the Blair bill in Congress.

Before leaving the condition of the South as to the education of its citizens, let us briefly inquire what the colored citizen himself has done in securing an education. He has done something, and yet much remains to be done. In this respect it may be claimed, without fear of successful contradiction, that the African Methodist Episcopal Church has done more in the self-education of the colored race than any other religious denomination. In South Carolina there is Allen University, officered and instructed by colored men, engaged in the instruction of colored youth exclusively, and the institution is supported and maintained by the colored citizens themselves. So likewise is Paul Quinn, of Texas, Morris Brown, of Georgia, and several others throughout the South. The Baptists are next in this advancement. In Selma, Ala., there is the Selma University, supported mainly by the colored people themselves, and officered and instructed chiefly by colored teachers. So likewise is the Baptist Seminary of Louisville, Ky. Added to all these are the following institutions carried on by State aid and Northern bounty, but exclusively for the colored race, viz: Claflin University, at Orangeburg, the Benedict Institute, at Columbia, Clark University, Atlanta, and others, too numerous to mention, throughout the South. What benefit has been derived from this education? I answer, from these institutions of learning have come teachers capable of instructing their own race, a condition essentially necessary until the rights and privileges are equally enjoyed by all, and the Negro's inherent inferiority be disbelieved by a large number of those of the

Caucasian race now engaged in teaching him. The Negro has proven himself in the South as in the North capable of the intellectual advancement of his white fellow citizen, in proportion to the advantages given him; and this brings me to the next proposition, which is the *social* condition of the South to-day, another topic to which I will briefly refer now, but more largely treat further on in these pages.

The condition of the past which kept separate the rich from the poor, the black from the white, the aristocrat from the peasant, is rapidly passing away under the influence of education, industry and a true christianity, and yet the barriers are not all broken down. An eminent Democrat once said to the writer: Sir, our motto is, "the greatest good to the greatest number." I replied then: Sir, the Negro ought not to have any fear of the amount of good he will get in the South, as his number is largest in that section, but I fear Democratic method of counting numbers at all times, to which reply he made no rejoinder. In the South the social condition is seen too in the relationship of capital to labor, or employer to employee, and in the equal enjoyment of civil privileges and industrial pursuits by all of its citizens alike. These relationships are not in harmony one with the other, and are the chief reasons why the prosperity of the South is not more advanced than it is. As regards capital and labor 75 cents per day for the laboring class of men, and 50 cents for women must grow a class of paupers in any community, and produce petty crime. This price of labor which prevails in the South, and which will not enable the poorer classes to provide for their families, in connection with the oppressive *lien* system are the chief causes of the recent exodus of colored laborers from the South. It is not politics, except as this method of poor wages is adopted to keep dependent the employee and thus control his vote. As regards the lien system which enables the small farmer to secure agricultural advances during the maturity of his crop, although ample protection is provided by law, yet the contrivances of the merciless merchant result in causing the lienor to find, at the end of the year, after paying his landlord's rent, or his fertilizing bill, then his lien for advances at 12 per cent. per month, that he is left not money enough to buy a hat, a pair of shoes, or a single garment of clothing for his family.

I cannot go farther into the details of this pernicious system, except to say it is sufficient to retard the progress of the South. It has lately so disturbed the social relations between employer and employee as to force the employer to use violence in obstructing and preventing, when he can, the emigration of his victims, thus setting at naught the absolute right of locomotion. This evil in South Carolina is sought to be remedied by the repeal of the lien law. The Negro is the principal victim of this robbery, and through the ignorance of a large part of the laboring class of this race they become an easy prey to this vicious cupidity.

Another social feature of the South which

blurs its progress and is a relic of the past, is the unjust discrimination of passengers on railroads. This arises from a prejudice of a Don Quixotic character, because the prejudice against color is about as sensible as Sancho's attack on the windmill. All nations at some time or other have had a species of caste prejudice, but none on the face of the globe has ever based it on color, save the American. How shall this ever change? First, it will change with the changed condition of the negro from dependent to equal, from ignorant to educated, from poor to the enjoyment of a competency, if not riches, and also with a changed condition of the Southern white man's mind and idea, that the Negro is by nature inferior, to a belief and a readiness to accept the daily proof before his eyes that he is a man and a brother, differing only in color of skin. To secure this recognition the colored man himself has something yet to do. He must not expect sympathy to advance him on the stage of life, he must not dally with opportunity, however small. He must not ask how to succeed; he must make success for himself by diligence. It is not thrift that is wanting, but economy on his part, and fair play from the white man. In this solution of the problem of the South, we must watch with care the means whereby the Negro will proportionately advance. And what are those means? First, unlimited opportunity; second, capacity and fitness; and third, action! I mean by action, a lively interest in advancing our condition. Let us be industrious. An economical industry gave to the Jewish people, the world over, a status among their persecutors never dreamed of. When the English people consented to tax the Jew in the time of the puerile John Lackland, and to make the penalty the extraction of a tooth for every dollar due, they little thought to see the day when the Rothschilds would control all Europe, financially; Disraeli would guide an empire so vast that upon its boundaries the sun never sets; or to listen to the erudition of one of Hebrew origin in the citadel of learning at Oxford. I firmly believe that like the Jew, the Negro will in the next century appear no mean factor in the economy of civilization. Already from chattledom he has advanced to manhood; from bondage to freedom; from a political serfdom to the rights of a citizen; from ignorance to a plane of learning and knowledge which astonishes his critics. Today in the "New South" he is the chief architect of his race's future. His position as freeman, as citizen, as lawyer, as doctor, as divine, as artist, as inventor, as farmer, as school teacher, as property holder, as followers of a true God, must produce that social status which the impartial mind of research has already discovered. Dr. Haygood has found it. Also our noble advocate, Mr. Cable, has declared it. Social status is not created in America out of blood and rank, as some believe, but is only the development of condition. And in this the Negro should not be measured from the "depths from which he has come, but the heights to which he has attained," as Mr. Frederic Douglass has truly remarked.

The pioneer of Southern thought on the new social condition is Mr. Geo. Cable, who clearly, forcibly and logically proves that social changes in the South must follow the development of the "New South." I will extend these views in the following pages.

And now let us look briefly at the political condition of the South. This, perhaps, is the worst feature of the "New South." The present political condition of the South is one which demands serious attention. The Democratic government of the South is a usurpation, as I have already said. It was wrested from the hands of a legitimate party by fraud and violence, and no Democrat of the South will deny this, but will excuse it on the grounds which have more than once presented themselves in countries for the necessity, as it is called, viz: reformation. But I ask what excuse can there be for usurpation in a republican form of government to ensure reformation? It may suit monarchies, despotisms and autocracies, but never a true democracy. In the South to-day the vote of a majority of its citizens is suppressed; it is true, not as heretofore, by violence, but in South Carolina there *is* the Procrustean Eight Box system, and in other States other devices to suppress the ballot of the Negro. It is claimed by the Democrats of South Carolina that this system of eight boxes only demands the intelligence of the voter. Even so, it is still but a device to nullify the ballot of the uneducated voter. It may not be legally wrong, but it is morally wrong, but I believe it is both. But this too must soon pass away. In the next ten years four-fifths of the voting population of the South will have received sufficient education to enable them to read their ballots. In a special chapter I shall more fully treat of this topic, except to state now that this is the result of Republican endeavor.

I concede the past grandeur of the Republican party. It saved a nation from ruin; it gave credit to the country of the greatest possibilities; it enacted principles which gave freedom to a race of people in bondage in its midst; it laid the foundations for the industry of millions; it planted schools and universities; it encouraged art and science; for twenty odd years it has held the helm of the nation so firm as to command the respect of the most powerful of its contemporaries. What then is the duty of the hour? It is to demand that the fundamental principles of our constitution shall be living, vitalizing powers in the South as in the North, and that every vote cast in the South shall be fairly counted—a free ballot and a fair count should be enforced.

I may have presented the bright side of the picture of the South in these general views at the expense of the dark. There are both sides in the South today, yet no one taking a retrospect of the past can fail to see progress under the influence of a new spirit in the South. But a short time ago a Southern editor, decrying the false idea that the Caucasian race would always hold sway over the Negro, exclaimed to his people, "*Hodie mihi cras tibi.*" Yes, there *is* a tomorrow for the Negro in the South, and all who see his progress in the short space of twenty years must recognize this. The day is near at hand when, as I believe, all race feeling will disappear, and a feeling which those who having a common interest must necessarily have—a common feeling must prevail. No other condition can exist in America while under the genius of true Republican principles. Unity will prevail in the "New South" when justice is done to black and white alike. God reigns; it must be so!

CHAPTER II.

THE SOUTH POLITICALLY.

In discussing this portion of the history of the South, as it relates to its political condition, I will commence at the new phase of political history brought about by the late civil war. One of the main features and consequences of the late civil war, was the political enfranchisement of the Negro. The contest between the North and South, which was decided by a clash of arms upon the battlefield, was the right of the South to maintain and extend slavery within certain boundaries. This simple issue soon drew to it numerous dependent issues, which enlarged the original stream into a large and powerful river. Among these dependent issues involved was the right of the Negro, enfranchised, to hold the political power of the ballot necessary to the maintenance of his freedom. The Reconstruction Acts of Congress were preparatory to the exercise of the elective franchise of the enfranchised Negro. Many and arduous were the struggles of noble hearted statesmen who sought the best means for their country's welfare. That the Negro as a freeman became an integral part of the body politic and was entitled to be governed only by his consent, could not easily be denied in accordance with our natural organic act, which says "that all just government rests upon the consent of the governed." But it still remained a question with many, how best and safest to reach this end. Some contended for an educational qualification for the newly enfranchised; others a property qualification; others a total denial of the ballot; and even when the ballot was given the Negro, many of the Southern States sought before reconstruction to nullify the same by acts such as were known in the State of South Carolina as the "Black Code." After reconstruction, and when it became evident that the Negro was a full-fledged voter, the question then arose what relation would he bear to his ex-master in his new role of voter and freeman. No one was better able to solve this problem than the ex-master himself. He well knew that the war had decided the fate of slavery and forever buried it in the oblivion of past ages, and that the Constitution of the United States had been decided to be the supreme law of the land; that the condition of every State that had engaged in rebellion re-entering the Union, was to regard this constitution as the supreme law of the land and to give paramount allegiance to the same. Yet many of these misguided men sought to solve the problem of the Negro's fitness as a voter by all sorts of persecution.

Let the reader refer to "Thorns in the Flesh," for much that is true as well as much that is false concerning this period of the South's history—Rifle Clubs, Ku Klux Klans, incendiaries, the burning of churches, the indescribable persecution of individuals; all characterized the entrance of the Negro as a voter upon the political arena in the South, until it became necessary to protect the Negro in the exercise of his suffrage, by the enforcement of his right at the bayonet's point. Some people hold up their hands in holy political horror when one asserts the right of the Federal Government to protect the voter in this method. Just as well declare unconstitutional the right of Congress to secure to every State a republican form of government. The Republican party has done all in its power to secure this form of government to the South—by planting schools therein to instruct the ignorant voter; and, next, by exercising Federal power, when necessary, to enable him to do so. The Freedmen's Bureau was an earnest of the good intentions of the National Government and of the Republican party at that time in power, not to thrust the ignorant unprepared, in the forum of civil government. But none will deny that the South turned its back upon this offer, and when asked for bread gave a stone. In 1868 the Republican party took control of the South, under the most favorable auspices, to maintain its power, ever before or since known to any party.

Behind them, and in front of them, and all around them, there was the Negro as a voter. How they used this support in shaping the political future of the South, should be investigated ere we can properly reach a true view of the

South politically. It cannot be denied that had many Northern white Republicans in the South so used the Negro vote as to make it a growing instead of a decreasing power, it would have kept the States in the Republican party until to-day.

But the Negro vote was used selfishly and in many instances insincerely. While friends at the North were trying to elevate the Negro of the South by education and christian teaching, the few demagogues who were in their midst were polluting the stream with avarice and political greed. In this condition the Negro was between the upper and nether millstones, and became nullified as a voter. It is said by some that the Negro voter of the South was led to vote the Republican ticket by Northern demagogues. This is a slander upon the Negro, whose political creed was one of solemn conviction and the preservation of rights bought with their blood. The condition of the South made it as natural for the Negro to be Republican as for the young of animals to follow their parents. The error was not in this, but in the neglect of those who controlled the Negro vote to elevate it; to make it a thinking and responsible power in the party, and not to be satisfied with sentiment.

The change in the political party of the South took place in 1876. The Southern Democrat claims it as the period of political reformation in the South. It was the reverse, for truly it was the period of political reformation at the

North. Some who had been our foremost advocates at the North, saw a herd of Republican office seekers and cried aloud with the Southern man to "Unload!" This was the beginning of the decline of the Republican party in the South. After nearly ten years of Rip-Van-Winkle sleep, the Democrats awoke to find themselves considered by the North, and the Republicans aroused, rubbed their eyes, to find out that *they* were condemned.

The political change of the South in 1876 was brought about by blood and murder, such as had not stained the annals of history since the Inquisition. But this, after all, may be a partizan view. Can political changes be brought about by force only? I think not. The condition which prepared the way for the Southern Revolution, was the American sentiment concerning the Negro. Flush with victory and enjoying the spoils of conquest, the Republican white ruler had rest contented with the black man and brother as a voter; but in course of time, as year added to year and he grew in intelligence, and leaders of the Negro race sprang up in the government of the States as well as the government of the United States, the question arose: "What shall we do with the Negro?" The answer came back: "*Unload!*" How then can it be said the Negro has forsaken the Republican party? The Supreme Court declared him not entitled to Federal protection in his civil rights as a citizen of the United States, but relegated him to the mercy of his Southern enemies, who from policy at least have dealt mildly with him although in their power. For had the South chosen to take this bludgeon of injustice and use it against the Negro, it might have reduced him to a condition worse than the Russian serf. It was the American sentiment of Negro inferiority as a race, not incapacity, that made the Southern Revolution of 1876 possible. But since 1876 the South, politically, has taken a new phase of government towards its citizens. The Negro voter is practically disfranchised. But the Democratic party says this is false—the Negro is free to vote. In reply I ask the question: If the Negro is free to vote, say in South Carolina, where his majority is indisputable, how does it come to pass that the Democratic party is in power and the Negro still Republican? Let us grant, as is true, that there are hundreds of Negroes who are Democrats, is it claimed that this accession has destroyed entirely the Republican majority? Not even the most ultra Democrat claims this. This is the true claim made in calmer moments, namely, it was *necessary* to defeat the Republican party to produce the necessary reformation needed in the South; to put a stop to ignorance controlling.

If this were true, the means used were radically wrong; education was the true remedy, not the shot gun. And this brings us to the question, "What is to be the political future of the South?" Its present is that of an oligarchy. The old remnant of slavocracy yet lives and now governs. Only a few have seen the light and would catch the sunshine of progress while they may. The parade of loyalty to the Union and yet questioning and resisting when they can its every Federal power, is yet in the South. The spirit of Phillips Brooks still stalks like a ghost in the United States Senate, shaking its fists at loyal men. But be not deceived; this is not the growing spirit of the South. In the next ten years, when the Negro and the white man are indeed each others peers as citizens, a new South will arise. But this time is retarded by the South itself—the old fogies which still live are so many barnacles to the ship "The New South." There needs in the South a leader who is abreast of the times—one who can see that capital and labor harmoniously at work prepare and support the strongest political government of the surest foundation, far more so than poverty and indolence. It is not so much how to prepare the Negro to be a useful peasant in the South, as it is to prepare him to be a useful citizen.

The present political government of the South resting as it does upon the consent of the few whose power is derived not from law but through intelligence and wealth, can only last as long as the soil in which it grows is capable of sustaining it, namely ignorance and poverty. When these fertile fields of Democratic usurpation are no more, and the masses of youth now comprising thousands and tens of thousands who are getting knowledge in schools and experience in the privileges of freedom arrive at maturity, the Democratic Othello who has lived upon tissue ballots, bullets and other means of political frauds, will lose his occupation. It cannot be supposed that when the majority of citizens of the South are educated—I mean the colored portion especially, that they will permit themselves to be governed without their consent as they are now, what avail will *then* the South Carolina eight-box system be when the voter can read and distinguish one box from the other? And again, the South must change, politically, for other and stronger reasons. The scars of the late civil war are fast healing—among some men of the South there is no vestige to be seen. They are thoroughly reconstructed; *action* and *progress* are their watchwords. Among others the *old cause*, and not as some call it, the *lost cause*, is yet cherished in their memory. With them stagnation and retrogression mark their every step. Now, although this latter class is in the majority, yet truth being stronger than error the minority prevails, and this accounts for the evident progress of the South in spite of its "Toombs," its Butlers and its Ben Hills. The introduction of capital and the emigration of new settlers, will make a political transformation never conceived of. This period is our necessary probation.

At present what is the political status of the South? You may travel its length and breadth and you will find a spirit of caste prejudice exercised towards a class of citizens known as Negroes, and their descendants. Our schools have improved in the past ten years as I have already said, but distinction and discrimination yet remain. The schools of white children are better provided for than those of the blacks, and this is not denied but excused on the ground that the white people pay more taxes than the colored. If the taxes are to be pro rated in their benefits through education, why not in other respects for which the taxes of the citizens go indiscriminately? Why not pro rate the amount of space in the public highway to be used by the colored and white citizens respectively? Why not pro rate the use of the police force—in its protection? Not only in the schools but in the administration of the government of the South there is caste prejudice. Our colored citizens are not even pro rated in the jury box, for while they are a majority at the polls, they find themselves a minority in the jury box. But I hear a Democrat say "We cannot lend ourselves to admit ignorance to govern." This is true, and no Democrat will find any honest and intelligent colored man who is not a demagogue denying that, but the question presents itself "Is the rule applied impartially?" Not at all. It is no unusual thing to find ignorant white men in the jury box and intelligent colored ones excluded. In my practice of law in South Carolina, I find it a rare thing that a prosecuting officer will admit a colored man to sit on a jury. Two or three are always impanneled to save a law question, but in the exercise of challenge for the State they are never allowed to go unchallenged. And it is a matter of observation that they will be excluded whenever the prisoner is a colored person, and not so frequently when it is a white person, as if the prejudice of the white man against the Negro is not as good a ground for excluding him from trying a Negro on the ground of bias or prejudice, as the love of the colored man for his race is good ground to exclude him on the ground of favorable bias.

But my own solution of this problem is that the white man of the South knows the colored man of the South in his weakness well. He has marked his vices and overlooked his virtues. He knows when he puts him upon a jury to try a white man that eleven white men can control him, and this is true frequently when even he sits to try one of his own. Then the reason why he is so discriminated against is to debase him; and the reason why colored men choose rather to be tried by a white jury, is a want of confidence in their own race. The ignorance of the colored citizen is the reason given by those who affect discrimination and injustice towards the Negro; but this answer will not do, because this evil prevails to an alarming extent among the whites as well, who are allowed to enjoy the privileges of government. It is an undeniable fact that in South Carolina so ignorant have been the white trial justices, until the white citizens cried out for a change. And in places where this ignorance exists, there are many intelligent colored men. But the politician says "the spoils to the victors." True; but call things by the right name and we will not complain. We complain against the garb of purity which the Democrat wears, while underneath there is so much hideousness. There is no denying the fact that a great change of mental development must the South undergo, ere it can attain the plane of a fair and impartial policy in the government of its citizens. This change must be brought about by the mental self-development of its citizens— black and white, and by the increase of capital, greater latitude for labor, the adequate pay of wages, the increase of industry and the spread of knowledge. These are the foundation stones upon which the superstructure of the "New South" is to be erected. Many honest Southern white men see this and would prepare for its advent; others are too blinded with prejudice to see even in the dim shadow of the future. Yet he who would observe the vast increase of knowledge in the South among the two classes which have hitherto been deprived of the benefits of education, must see the "New South" fast approaching. From these premises I predict that the present policy of Southern government cannot last longer than twenty years, when its sturdiest form as now existing will disappear.

The idea that the South has already worked a thorough change of political feeling, and that the wounds of the late civil war are healed and beyond recognition, is false. It was not so with any conquered people upon the face of the earth; it cannot be so with the Southern whites. The "lost cause" is not a forgotten cause; and the principles of an indissoluble Union of inseparable States, needs as greatly to be protected today by loyal principles among loyal Northern men, as it did twenty years ago. Who can fail to discern this in the speeches of Jefferson Davis, as delivered in Atlanta, Macon and Savannah, Ga., and Montgomery, Ala., and the reception they met from the Southern white people in whose ears they were uttered. What we need today is a stronger adherence to Republican principles, and less apology for them; a stronger maintenance of Republican laws, and less apostacy and truckling to Southern supremacy, until every citizen in America can not only boast in word but in deed, in every clime in the civilized globe upon which he may put his foot, that "I am an American citizen;" otherwise the American republican form of government must remain weak, and every wind and storm of political dissension which arises must shake it from its very foundation. The present work of the South is to prove the righteousness of its lost cause. There is not a Southern Congressman in Congress who has not this at heart as the work of his life. If this cause be righteous, let it prevail; if not, why trifle with it? Unity, peace and concord, cannot be purchased at the sacrifice of truth. Then with a firm determination to perpetuate the principles of the forefathers of our great government, let North and South, black and white, and every element of our cosmopolite nationality, study the Declaration of Rights in our incomparable Constitution, making it our political guide in peace;

our anchor and port of safety in times of war—civil or foreign; our talisman in our relationship with our fellow citizens, and the safety of the Republic is assured.

The important question which arises concerning the "New South," politically, is whether it shall inaugurate a new form of government contrary to the spirit and letter of the Constitution of the United States. In other words, shall the South be allowed to elect its representatives to both houses of Congress by methods which are frauds upon the rights of every other citizen in the North, East and West? Since it appears that thousands of voters in the South are deprived of the efficacy of their votes when cast, or denied the right to vote by fraudulent methods, then is the Southern Representative in Congress, when thus elected a Federal Representative as he should be, or even a State Representative in Congress? Whom does he represent? It is not the whole people of his State, for there are many who were not allowed to register their assent or dissent as to his election. It is not the assent alone of a majority of voters at an election for a candidate which makes a man a representative of his constituents, but also the right of the minority to pass upon his election. We are here supposing his election to be by a majority of voters, which in the South is not true.

This condition of affairs as at present exists in the South, is as much a usurpation as when one regent is driven from his throne by force and his place taken by another without right. When a question arises in Congress, it is by reason of its situation a national question always, and is supposed to be one affecting the whole people relatively. A Southern vote upon it affects Massachusetts as well as Texas. A representative, therefore, who has no right to a voice in that body is a usurper of the people's rights in Massachusetts as well as in Texas. If it be a question of taxation pertaining to a State, the vote is one which represents adversely that principle upon which our government was founded, viz: taxation without representation. This is a vital question pertaining in its effects to all the States of the Union, and no side or less important issue should be allowed to eclipse it.

Among the effects of this Southern usurpation, is the denial of the right to the colored citizen to representation, by and through his consent; and every colored voter, Democrat or Republican, should resist the innovation. As at present situated, the colored voter in the South is a political nondescript. Let him rise in his might, and demand this right which is his just due as an American citizen. This question ought to be considered irrespective of party politics or economics or social status. It relates to the future permanence of our republican form of government. Associate the disposition of some Americans to disregard the fundamental principles upon which our republican institutions are founded, with the rapid tendency of a large class of foreigners to establish disorder and anarchy in our midst, and see how long the American Republic will last under such conditions. The principles of no political party are better adapted to secure the permanence of republican institutions, than those of the Republican party.

CHAPTER III.

THE NEW SOUTH POLITICALLY.

This phase of the South is perhaps one of the most difficult to decide. How much the South is changed in its views politically from "Old" to "New," is not easily ascertained. "States Rights," or as sometimes called, "States Sovereignty," was, as is generally known, the chief cause of the civil war. It was not the approximate cause, but the remote cause of the war. The doctrine of the famous statesman of South Carolina, Mr. Calhoun, as exemplified in the nullification measures, was the fruit of the tree of State sovereignty. It gave a new impulse to the South to look upon itself as an independent government, disregarding the power of the Federal government. How far this idea is changed in the "New South," is difficult to tell. The assertions of today are loud and many, that the South is in harmony with the doctrine of the Union of States, but no careful observer can fail to see by acts and words that the South yet believes in its power to control measures, however federal in their nature, which it believes local in their relationship. The great hindrance to the passage of the Blair bill, a measure as I have already said more calculated to perpetuate the existence of the Republic than millions of treasure, is caused by that party in power at the time of my writing, which is significantly the party of the South—I mean the Democratic party; and so long as it remains in power, with the idea of State sovereignty unchanged, we must look for this disastrous hindrance to the spread of education.

Neither has the South changed politically in denying political rights to fellow citizens on account of color or past condition of servitude. Despite freedom has shown to this portion of our country its vast benefits, and in spite of the constitutional laws which give the right of suffrage to every citizen, a large class of voters is deprived of the free, fair and just exercise of this privilege to vote. Despite high-sounding phrases in the platforms of this party in political conventions assembled, such as the following, to be found in the Democratic platform of 1884: "The Democratic Party of the Union recognizes that as the nation grows older, new issues are born of time and progress, and old issues perish. * * * * We hold that it is the duty of the government in its dealings with the people, to mete out equal and exact justice to all citizens of whatever nativity, race, color or persuasion—religious or political." I say in spite of this high-sounding language of the Democratic party, hundreds and thousands of citizens are at every succeeding election deprived of their right to vote upon no other ground than color. And since then, as before, hundreds of this same class of persons have fallen victims to injustice by the hands of lawless men, forming a court of "Judge Lynch," and taking vengeance into their own hands for alleged crimes, in the face of legally organized courts and their machinery, established for the orderly and civilized trial of persons accused of crimes.

From 1872 to 1876, the South took into its hands the right to govern, control and determine all political elections according to its conceived idea of the "white man's right to control government." Where this strange political doctrine derives its validity, except in the brains of fanatics, is hard to conceive. In order to establish this doctrine and maintain it, the political organizations known as Ku Klux Clubs were organized, and their deeds are too well known to the American reader to need repeating here, except to state that they were brutal, and their existence a stain upon the free institutions of American government. It is but just to say, that this method of controlling elections has partially ceased since 1876, because, as events show, the necessity no longer exists—*cessante ratione cessat lex*. The party of Ku Kluxism is in power by the weakness of a great national government, whose constitution declares in Art. IV, "The United States shall guarantee to every State in this Union a republican form of government," etc.; and yet this National or Federal power declares itself, through its judicial, legislative and executive voices, im-impotent to perform its contract with the people, for a State is an aggregation of people organized for civil purposes, chief among which is the protection of the ballot, or in other words, allegiance for the protection given, and termed contract between people and the government. The new method of the South is endeavor how best to deprive the voter of color of the effect of his vote. In South Carolina various are the devices, but none more transparent than that known as the "Eight Box System." This prescribes the necessity for every voter to be able to read his ballot and deposit it in the right box. This upon its face is but the just privilege of every State to protect itself in its government from the evils of ignorance, and no patriot can or should complain of the exercise of this protection.

But the South politically is unjust. It discriminates at the polls, in the jury box, and in the halls of legislation. The colored voter is deprived of the exercise of these privileges upon the specious ground of ignorance, while the white voter is winked at in his ignorance, so long as he is engaged in oppressing his colored fellow citizen. I well remember as a lawyer, sitting in court at Orangeburg, S. C., shortly after the Democratic usurpation of 1876, and witnessing the organization of a petit jury. When the list of jurors was read by the clerk of the court and each juror had answered to his name, and the panel for trial was formed, it was found to consist of seven white and five colored men. This greatly incensed the Court, in that even a minority of colored men should be on the jury; and the judge presiding, who was formerly a

Republican, but seeing no further political favor from his old party soon became a Democrat, delivered a philippic on the ignorance of the Negro and his unfitness to take part in the administration of the government and then called upon the clerk to name one of the seven white jurors to preside as foreman of the jury, when to his Honor's astonishment and chagrin, all seven alternately excused themselves upon the plea that they could neither read nor write; whereupon the clerk called upon the "brother in black," and found three who could both read and write. Yet the practice of appointing a white man as foreman of a jury, exists in nearly all parts of the South, and despite the great majority of Negroes in the South, and the statutory provisions of an indiscriminate choice of electors as jurors, still today two or three is the greatest number of colored jurors ever to be found in most of the Southern States; and the Negro's participation in the administration of the government in any of these departments, is limited almost beyond mention. Hence it must appear from all these facts, that the South is not new politically.

But the advocates of the South say it is preparing to be a new South politically, by educating the Negro and the ignorant poor white; and there are many, as I have aforesaid, who are faithfully trying to prepare the way for this new path. Indeed, it is apparent to many Southern whites, who are not too stubborn to learn of the new issues born, that the Negro is an important factor in the South, politically as well as industrially, and that no force can destroy or annihilate him; and that it is better to prepare him for citizenship and its privileges, than to deny him these rights. Again, many see that the Negro is now a thinking voter like his fellow white citizen and not an automaton; it is now with him, *homo sum ergo cogito*. The South is new, in that it begins to seek the Negro vote. Unable much longer to uphold party power by bloodshed and force, it will cultivate the Negro voter's adherence. But can the Negro be a Democrat so long as Democracy denies him his civil and political rights? I answer, no! Not until the Democratic party upholds Republican principles by practising justice and equality to the Negro in the South. Meanwhile let the Negro take care not to follow the shadow of *any* party while its substance is withheld from him. Let the Republican party treat fairly the Negro, and let the Democratic party abandon its paths of distinction and violence and injustice towards him because of his color, and then let the Negro as a freeman choose between them. This is to be the "New South" politically, perhaps not during the present generation, but surely in the generation to come. At present for the Negro the Republican party is his only shelter—the roof under which he can find protection under the law for his rights as a citizen. To enter the Democratic household with the shotgun, the rifle club, the hangman's rope on the wayside tree, the ballot box stuffer, the convict system and the like in the South, is not the mark of wisdom, even though the invitation be kind and earnest.

The middleman in each political party recommends that the Negro voter in the South should go to the Democratic party as a measure of safety for himself, peace to the South and general prosperity. Although having as great a desire as anyone to see the harmonious relation of the two races consummated, I cannot recommend what seems a surrender of manhood. That the Negro voter of the South or elsewhere should have to enter the Democratic party as a measure of *safety*, is to purchase at the cost of his manhood what the constitution ought to secure him by *law*. More than this, it is to seal his fate as a political serf. It is easy to see that if the Democratic party knows that the Negro is a Democrat because he fears Democratic persecution, this fear will be kept up to keep him in the party. This I think may easily be seen by the Negro citizen the whole United States over, in seeking the party where his rights are best protected. Is this safety to be found in the Democratic party? Let the colored citizen decide for himself. The history of the two parties should be consulted for a fair answer. In the light of progress and civilization, chief among whose elements is education, it is easy to perceive that the colored voter will not be chained to any party from sentiment. Like other voters he will and should consult his best interests not as an individual as many do, but as an integral part of a race whose rights and privileges are yet denied in the enjoyment in common with his fellow white brethren. To enter the Democratic party to beg for our rights and protection, is cowardly and unwise; and so long as that party adheres to the belief that the political rights of the Negro should be abridged, it is not the party for the Negro of the present day. The time may come when the eyes of Democracy will be opened to the justice and equality of rights for the Negro, but in the light of existing events in the South, the time has not yet come. But some say to enter the Democratic party and become a part of it, is to force a change of heart. I have no objection to those who would undertake the task. It is worth a trial, and no man should be condemned for trying what he believes he can do. There must be pioneers for every undertaking and many must die in the cause and for the cause's sake. There are no cultivated fruit trees from which you can gather fruit in the land of the pioneer; no smooth pathways, but rugged roads; no tame animals, but the fierce tiger and lion. These our colored Democratic friends must encounter in the work of reform upon which they say they have entered. But the work will be accomplished in the South only, under new influences, new laws, new ideas and new industries; and not by a million colored citizens voting any particular ticket, now or ever.

CHAPTER IV.

THE SOCIAL PROBLEM OF THE SOUTH.

In continuation of my views as expressed in the foregoing pages, I will now call attention to that status of the South just prior to, and since the late civil war, in which it finds itself, as to the social relationship of its people, consisting of the two races, distinguished by their color—black and white, in its midst.

I speak of the social condition of the South, not so much from the standpoint of civil government, as from what may be termed its civic-domestic government, or, in other words, society from its primal aspect, as first viewed in the home, and more ordinary intercourse with man and his fellow, unrestricted, except in an indirect manner, by the civil law. All just powers of popular government are derived from the consent of the people, who give up their primal rights of self, individual government, in accordance with and in proportion to their necessity for obtaining the profit to be derived from organized government. Notwithstanding all this, there is always remaining in a people an inherent self-government, which always develops itself in proportion to the energy, industry, morality and civilization of said people, which may be styled social development, and which forms the substratum of social government, which is the foundation of all legal government. And just in proportion to the civilized development of a people, of a society or class, so is the extent, strength, beauty and justice of its legal superstructure—government. As is the tree, so will be its fruit—as borne by its branches. When one desires to inquire into the causes of development or non-development of a people or race or class of people, it is best to first inquire into the component parts of the society which comprise such people, their manners, customs and habits, for which laws are enacted to regulate, but which precede all law, and become the *causa causans* of all law and government. It is then with this view before us, and these fundamental propositions, that we shall examine first the social condition of the South in regard to the relationship and intercourse of its people and races, one with the other, their manners, customs and habits, and the problem or question for the best means for the solution of the development of this section of our country from the standpoint of its present social condition. The future development of no people has ever been properly prognosticated, except through their social condition; and I think a careful analysis of the social condition of the South, will do more to open the eyes of its people and their advocates to their needs for advancement, peace and prosperity, than legislation or excited public or private discussion.

We shall therefore commence with the social condition of the South just prior to the civil war, which, among its many effects, uprooted and totally destroyed the former social condition of the South, as markedly as did the flood of 6,000 years ago disturb and disarrange the physical arrangement of the earth's strata, as compared before the flood. Before the war, the social condition was especially marked by the relationship of master and slave, rich and poor, a condition, as I have aforesaid, very much like the feudal system in France and England in the 10th century, save in that the service due the master in America was menial and involuntary, and in nowise of a military character, or in return of any allegiance due the master for the protection received by the servant or slave. The effect of the social condition of master and slave, as it existed in America, in the South especially, was to keep one class of people rich and another poor; one class informed and another ignorant; one class in the light of morality, the other in the darkness and degradation of superstition and sin; one class as capable of enjoying the advantages of exercising their talents in industry and enjoying the privileges of all advancement in knowledge, in learning, art and science; the other class as enduring physical labor, without any mental development thereby. These two divisions of conditions were occupied by what was known as the aristocratic whites or slave-holders, and the poor whites and the Negro or slave. During this condition the South grew not in industrial advancement. Its citizens, instead of being owners of ships and factories, and engaged in developing the rich mineral resources of their lands, fostering a varied commerce with the civilized portions of the earth, cherishing the arts and sciences and establishing schools for the education of all its citizens, chose rather to be satisfied with slave-labor in the production of cotton only, and to restrict the knowledge of science and art, and the possession of useful learning to the few, who were the sons and daughters of rich land-owners, who were generally also slave-owners.

The common public school was a thing unknown in the times of slavery. The college opened its doors only to the rich few. The private school was little observed. It was a social precept among the slave-owners, to keep the poor whites and the slave, who was the Negro, in ignorance and mental darkness. This estrangement and division kept apart not only the two races of people in the South, but divided the whites themselves into rich and poor, ignorant and educated. The picture as it presents itself to the eye of memory today is: the white slave-owner in his lordly palace, with all the luxuries of life flowing in from the toil of others, becoming torpid in mind, body and estate for the want of a just competition, a necessity for active energy in procuring the wants of life. There was the middle man, too, as an overseer or agent, who lorded it over the slave, only in turn to be lorded over by the slave-owner. The effect which this condition had upon capital was to keep it circumscribed, and its accumulation a mere stagnant pool of wealth. The labor of the slave enriched the master, and kept poor the slave. Slave labor was the substitute for machinery in the art of agriculture, and in nowise was this labor used to improve mentally the laborer. Land was almost inalienable—in fact there was no one to buy. The wages of the poor whites were kept within a mere subsistence, and of course to the slave there was no compensation. Trades were taught the slave only as a means of profit to his owner, a privilege which the poor whites only enjoyed in a small degree.

In the South, even during slavery, there were two classes of colored persons known, the "free colored person" and the slave. These free colored persons either never were slaves, they being free men from the West Indies or other parts of the globe, or were from the North, where slavery had been abolished in the larger portion of the States. This distinction was another feature in the social condition of the South, and divided it into slave-owner, or rich white generally; poor white, free colored persons and slaves. These classes were separate and distinct in manners, habits and customs, and the effects of such distinction remain even today. The slave-owner, as the sole possessor of all rights, both of the slave, free colored man and the poor white, had no fear from these classes. He was a man who did not need to improve in industry, because there was no necessity; the poor white saw no hope in his improvement, as *he* was regarded as a social inferior; the slave's case seemed definitely fixed; and the free colored man, was a kind of nondescript, being neither free nor slave. His position was one more of irritation than of peace, although he knew it not nor was responsible for it. These social barriers and distinctions produced a social condition such as was exemplified in all the habits, customs and manners of the people. The slave-owner in his lordly castle, with every comfort surrounding him, all rights secured and all privileges obtained. Opportunity, leisure and wealth, secured him the way to advancement. The slave-owner's God was one of his own interpretation and belief, very much as it is even today with his successors. He reasoned not from nature to nature's God, but from an unknown source or cause to all the effects which he beheld.

The individual aspect of the slave's condition and that of the poor white man, was seen in their houses, which were log cabins and other humble huts; their food of a scanty and proscribed order; their dress of the simplest but poorest style and quality. There was a total absence of the rules which govern supply and demand, as labor from the blacks was involuntary, and from the poor whites controlled by an illegal power in the hands of the capitalist. But despite this, there was still a more fearful condition of the social relationships as it related not to the slave and the free colored man, but to the poor white man. These two classes, which were termed the lower order of society, readily found a distinction among themselves and a difference between each other. A poor white man was of no esteem in the eyes of an aristocratic white man, who frequently openly showed this difference between a slave and a poor white man, in favor of the former and against the latter. This further produced a social difference between the pet slave and the poor white man, with this in favor of the poor white, that he was free. Moreover, the example set by the slave-owner, that slavery was the normal condition of the slave, taught the lowest white man that his skin was a premium upon which he could alone rely. *Sans* brains, culture or property, to try and oppress the Negro. There was never, therefore, any true harmony between the races in the South, in no condition of social life. For more than two hundred years ago this condition as I have described existed, until it began to enter not only the social, but the religious, domestic and political condition of the people; and in this social condition did the South find itself at the commencement of the civil war. It was a social condition ill calculated to benefit or advance a people or a section of our country. And from this condition it does not seem reasonable to believe the oft repeated assertion, that had the South put the slaves into the battlefield, they would have secured victory against the Union. The strength of any people lies in a community of interest—a oneness of purpose, a common benefit to be derived. Could this be believed by any slave, even in his ignorance, had he been put in the field by slave-owners?

At the close of the war a new social condition arose necessarily under new circumstances and new influences. The war in its effect gave liberty to four million of human beings formerly known as slaves, a condition in which they were regarded as property and hence could not own even themselves. The severest effect of the war upon the South, from a Southern standpoint, was the levelling of the social status of its people as citizens in common. The riches of the slave-owner had vanished, generally. The slave was no longer a chattel but a free man—his labor was now his own; and in this he became a competitor in life with his former master, with the great disadvantage on the slave's side of ignorance and inexperience. During slavery the land of the South was entirely possessed by the slave-owner and constituted his riches as well as did his slaves. When these latter became free, nothing was left the Southern white man but his land, which in right belonged in a large proportion to the slave. Land held by a slave-owner was like land held by one man, who purchases it with the money of another but takes title in his own name. The law says such a holder of land is but a trustee for the owner of the money, and the land if alienated to a purchaser with notice, is the land of the money owner. Is not this like unto land held by a slave-owner, with the unrequited labor of the slave? From this view confiscation would have been equity to the slave and justice from a government to which he had been loyal. But the facts are, that the slave at the close of the war had only muscle and the right to labor, and be compensated for his labor, and the slave-owner his land and the right to utilize it.

There was but little ready money in the South at the close of the war. It would appear that from this point there was a new start in life for both black and white, and that the laws of supply and demand would hereafter regulate the social intercourse between the races in the South, as protected by just and humane laws, should be expected. The two chief elements of social progress were at hand—muscle and land. These were the only ones existing from the creation, until Abraham introduced the system of barter between himself and Lot. They are the true sources of human advancement, upon the basis of equal opportunity. There may seem no practicable way at this time of the civilization of man to put in practice Henry George's possession in common of all property, but the more practical plan of an equal share of profit between capital and labor from a primitive start, did certainly present itself at this period. But there existed an inequality, which wherever it exists produces oppression and injustice, namely, the inequality between knowledge and ignorance. At the close of the war, the ex-slaves were all ignorant, the slave-holder was educated, and despite the political change of government which gave power in legislation to the ex-slave, he was yet in a large measure controlled by his former master, as he is in a great degree even today.

The laws which were enacted to protect the slave were evaded and of little benefit, through the advantage of education in the hands of the master. Let us illustrate: the master having but little capital, save as represented by his hundreds of acres of lands, had to contract with the new freeman for his labor to work it. Sometimes this contract was evidenced by writing; more frequently it was oral, and although the National Bureau of Education was set up in the South to protect him in his labor as well as to give the enfranchised education, it frequently happened that little protection was afforded the slave through it, because many used their positions to elevate themselves to office rather than the ex-slave to learning. There were few men of the Freedmen's Bureau who carried into the work that faithfulness and true love for the elevation of the poor Negro, as did the philanthropist, Major-General Howard. If all had been so, education had been more thoroughly and widely obtained by the freedmen, and his advancement greater than at present. But instead of this, the contract of the slave for wages, or as purchaser of land or personal property, was well nigh always proven to be worthless when sought to be carried into effect, because of his want of education. If an ex-slave entered into a contract to work land or to buy a mule, or a small farm, he was furnished with a writing (sometimes there was no evidence in writing), or he relied on a verbal promise to fulfil said contract, which at the time of fulfillment was either denied by the educated master as having been entered into, or perverted from its original intent by ingenuity in the ex-master.

It is said the Negro of the South is thriftless. It is not true. This is seen in his progress, which I shall more specifically refer to hereafter. But let us see the causes of his present condition, as compared with his white fellow citizen. I need but say that he is immeasurably inferior in wealth. The capital produce of the South, as we all know, is cotton, the producing of which is almost entirely performed by Negro labor. The quantity of cotton produced since the war, by the hands of the freeman, is well nigh twice as much as that produced by the slave. From this fact there ought to be a fair proportion of progress between the ex-master and the ex-slave, despite the disparity in knowledge; but what do we find? Why today the ex-master is vastly wealthier than the laboring freeman. And what are the causes of this great disparity? I answer, poor wages, bad laws and race prejudice, arising from social distinction. These three combined have produced the present social condition of the South. Since the war, the wages paid to the laboring blacks and poor whites have been such as to keep them both in a constant state of peonage. At the close of the war, added to the renting of small farms to the colored man by whites, to be paid in certain proportions of the crop, was the system of making advances to this class of farmers of such necessary farming utensils and necessities for food and clothing, as would enable them to produce said crop. This system in its incipiency had nothing in its intent discommendable, but it afterwards grew into the strongest engine of power, political and civil, as turned against the colored laborer and the poor white. The profit to be derived from such an occupation, in which total ignorance had to compete with panoplied intelligence, soon caused numerous small merchants, as grocers and vendors of other articles, to set up small stores on every plantation cultivated. In most instances the merchant was also landlord, and in this combination commenced a system of usury, unrivalled by the Jews of Lombardy in ancient times. The poor, ignorant colored and white man, renting small farms and relying on the merchant for advances to make his crop, were and still are compelled to pay the exorbitant interest, frequently of fifty per cent. and not unusually of seventy or ninety per cent. A coat which cost the merchant one dollar, was frequently sold for two; a pound of meat that cost six cents, was sold for twelve; a hat which cost fifty cents, was sold for $1.50; so likewise with shoes and other things. Few men having families were able to meet so great a burden, and those who did found nothing left as surplus from which they could in turn become capitalist like unto their employer. For, as Henry Ward Beecher truly says, speak- of capital and labor : "They are one under a new form. The capitalist is the laborer under circumstances, and when the laborer earns his dollar, he is a capitalist to all intents and purposes." This is as it ought to be, but it was not so in the South at the close of the war, and is not so today. I have seen colored men who, having a large family, rent a small farm and take advances for a year to make a crop, and at the end of said year, after paying such debts to the merchant as were incurred in making said crop, not have money enough to buy a suit of clothing for any one of the family. I have also seen the taking of all the crop by the merchant, and also, the horse or mule and other chattels which were given as collateral security for the debt in making a crop in one year. And, added to this, was the practice of either refusing to sell lands to the colored farmer, or, when contracting to do so, cheating him in the end by some artifice or design. The lands now possessed by the colored people of the South, are possessed in spite of the effort to keep them from becoming land-owners. I believe it to have been the early purpose of the ex-slave-owner, who was the land-owner of the South, to keep the freedman from owning the soil and becoming educated, knowing that these two elements control government, when possessed by any class of people, and that, too, without regard to color or past condition. They well know that the political power obtained as a result of the conquest in war would not be permanent, nor could it withstand the power of capital against labor. The majority of the people being Negroes, it was necessary to keep this class poor and dependent. The poor laborer's political will is yet manacled by his employer, the capitalist, and he is asked to bow or starve. The laborer knowing that he is solely dependent on the capitalist for sustenance, is moved as he is moved; his will is scarcely his own; his judgment is decidedly under control. This belittling condition is the result of the oppression of capital against labor.

The outgrowth of this oppression is to establish two classes, a superior and inferior one in the South, as it is in the North, East and West, with this difference, that in the South the social condition is largely characterized by the caste prejudice of former condition and color, and this enters into and shapes laws and prescribes an ostracism. It is the land power in the South that makes back seats for Negroes in theatres and hotels, on railroad cars and in steamboats, nay, even in churches. It is capital that keeps the poor white man of the South and the Negro in a state of servitude, and affords but comparative improvement on their side, turn it and twist it as you may. It is capital as represented chiefly by land which makes murder in the South by a white man towards a Negro insanity; but when perpetrated by the Negro it is the "unlawful killing of a human being with malice aforethought." This inequality in the administration of justice lies deep in the social condition of the South. "A just and efficient government," says Walker, in his "Wealth of Nations of the State," "is important to realize the largest development of wealth." This unequal condition of affairs compels the question to be asked, is labor inferior to capital, since production lies at the base of all progress? Not at all. Yet we find that the effect of this unequal growth of material is to drive the people of the South into dual parts, like unto the feudal times of the lord and the peasant.

This unequal condition, arising from unequal advantages given to all classes in the South, has not only produced an aristocratic and peasant class, but it has obstructed industry and stunted the true development of the South. Southern white men have clung to farm life as the liveliest remembrance of the days of slavery. It keeps their former slaves near them and in a condition of dependence little better than the past, and the inequality produced by the difference between capital and labor, is seen in every ramification of social life in the South. It is the reason for the rude hut inhabited by one class and the kingly palace by another, for the possession of gold by one and rags by another, for the intellectual advancement of one class and the ignorance of another; in fine, it is the reason for the riches for one class of people and the poverty of another. This will always be while capital and labor are so unjustly related to each other. Mr. Henry George, both in his "Social Problems" and his more excellent work on "Progress and Poverty," describes these causes more clearly than any other political economist known to me. I may not be able to see clearly the adaptability of his unique and modern doctrine of tax on land, but it is true, as he says, that it is clear beyond dispute that the hitherto politico-economic methods laid down by others for regulating supply and demand, production and consumption, and the adjustment of capital to labor, has proven before-existing facts both inapplicable and ineffective.

We find this truth as laid down by Mr. George in his book on "Progress and Poverty" clearly evidenced in the social condition of the South, namely, "That wages, instead of being drawn from capital, are in reality drawn from the product of the labor for which they are paid," and the question put by him, "Why, in spite of increase of productive power, do wages tend to a minimum which will give but a bare living," is especially applicable to the present social condition of the South, while it is not wholly inapplicable, as we all know, to the likewise social condition of the North. There was never a time since "Adam delved and Eve span" that man and his fellow had so nearly an equal start in the two forces of production than when, at the close of the war, the ex-slave owner and the enfranchised slave started out, one with the representative of capital, viz: land, and the other the representative of production in labor—muscle. These two forces were the prime actors in making a new social condition for the South at the close of the late civil war; and now, after more than twenty years exercise of these forces, what is the result? Does it appear as if the law of supply and demand has been justly observed or was truly applied? Is it true that the progress of the South, which I have shown to have taken place, has improved the social condition of the South? Is it true that the Negro of the South, which is known as largely the laboring class, and, therefore, the producing class, has improved in *his* social condition compared with the white class, which is known as largely the capital or non-producing class? Why is it, in plainer terms, that the Negro who was poor at the close of the war when made free, is today yet poor when compared to the white man of the South? You may say that this is the result of the ignorance of the one and the knowledge of the other, but while I do not deny that ignorance and knowledge enter largely into the producing and non-producing quality of material advancement, it has not, and should not, have anything to do with the just relationship between capital and labor and the just wages paid as compensation for adequate labor.

None will deny that the labor in quality required for making cotton in the South is fully adequate to the need of producing the same, and this is seen in the fact that the cotton produced in the South since the war has greatly exceeded the amount produced before the war; and yet the producing power makes no material progress as compared with the non-producing power. I can see no other reason for this, than because capital has been, and still is, unjust to labor in the South as in a degree it is in the North, added to which there has been a greater degree of caste prejudice on account of color and former condition in the

South, blocking the avenues to industry and progress. As I have said before, it is not only the political change in the administration which is daily causing thousands of colored farm hands, and even mechanics, to migrate from the South to the West, but it is also caused by unjust wages, wages which do not admit of a bare living, such as 15 cents a day, and $6 or $8 per month. These low wages is carrying out the plan, said to have been suggested by Calhoun, for the purpose of "keeping the Negro down." And how is this done in the South? Not only by paying him poor wages and giving him poorer rations, but still further denying him the opportunity for material advancement. A colored man in the South cannot purchase land with the facility of his white brother, not only because of his poor wages as compensation for his services, but because of the general indisposition to sell him land. Since the war, thousands of colored people who have commenced to purchase lands have been unable to do so and have lost what they have already paid, not only because some were defaulters in payment, but because more were the victims of the white man's original design to defraud him by some clause in the mortgage or fee simple deed, which defeated his tenure just at the time when he thought most sure he was the absolute owner. I have in mind a few instances, which I will now give.

Nine colored men in the town of Orangeburg were sold 243 acres of land in several proportions.

Each regarded himself as a several contractor, and not purchasers in common; and when seven had fully paid their several shares and demanded the title deeds, they were told that they were joint purchasers, and the other two being defaulters the seven had to lose their payments, their improvements and their lots, and begin anew, heart broken and full of despair. Many had purchased, as they thought, fee simple estates in their lands from white men, when, at the death of the vendor, they found they had only been sold the life interest of the vendor. Others have purchased lands only to find in a few years a swarm of heirs arriving to maturity and, not joining in the original sale, claim their acquired interest in said lands. Some have mortgaged their property, say, for illustration, for $75, to find at the time of payment that the mortgage read $175, or $275, or $375. Among farm hands the pernicious system of liens, in which, as I have already referred, is a corroding poison to the very vitals of material progress of the colored farmer and the poor whites. For a pound of meat originally costing 6 cents the buyer has to pay 12 or 15 cents, a large percentage on his fertilizer, heavy cost for his apparel, and a heavier rent for his poor land. The law giving a preferred lien on the crop to the landlord after payment to him and attachment on the remainder by the lienee, the producer is left penniless and without legal protection by way of exemption from the stripping process of taking every pound of cotton and every grain of corn in his barn.

This system of discrimination between labor and capital, as seen in unjust wages and no protection, is also to be found among the few mechanics who perform operative labor in the South. It is not an unusual thing to see a white and a black mechanic, who although doing the same work, yet receive different wages. Discrimination is introduced even into the precincts of the schoolhouse. A first-class colored teacher never receives the equal salary of a first-class white teacher, a practice which, upon its face, carries with it the purpose of seeking inferior teachers for one class and superior for another. The professional, on account of caste prejudice, is shut out from equal opportunity of securing an equal patronage with his white fellow, because of his color. But added to all this is the further obstruction to social progress, as seen in the closing of the doors of industry, few as they are in the South, to the colored brother because of his color, and shutting them against him in every vocation in life which is not strictly menial. How then can the social condition of the South be other than a dividing and a divergent one between the races? And the question here arises, is the present social condition of the South one of true progress—materially or socially? I unhesitatingly answer, no! The South's progress, socially, is only apparent and shadowy; it is not substantial; it cannot be with a divided and unequal people in condition and opportunity.

The present social condition of the South, as

found in its white and black population, arises not so much from the habit of keeping separate these two classes on account of race or color, as by reason of the disparity in conditions and the hindrance to industrial pursuits set up by the same powerful whites against their weaker brethren—the blacks. You may say this is equally so with these two classes in the North, East and West, and yet the social condition is not the same. The principle is not different, but the facts are, and only serve to prove the truth of the principle. In the North, East and West, the largest number is the white class, and the result is in the order of the inverse ratio.

It cannot be denied that the social condition of the South in which it finds itself so far behind the other portions of our country in industry, is owing to the folly of keeping out from engaging in industrial pursuits the class of people largest in numbers in its midst. The folly of trades unions, or the spirit which denies colored persons admission to the workshops in the South, is the chief cause of Southern depression in trade, and despite the progress it has made, is the reason it has not made greater progress. It is evident that if the South could receive into its midst a large amount of capital, and would then open its avenues of industry for the large quantum of labor it possesses, in the large number of colored people in its midst, it would spring into a powerful, rich and more prosperous portion of our country, with magic and alacrity, and would be the garden spot of these United States. It possesses the resources—it only needs the development and the application of all the means to the said development. This discriminating process in the use of available labor, is the curse of every spot on which it is found. It has its origin in what is known in America as "trades unions," whose ostensible object is to protect labor against the oppression of capital, but whose hidden purpose is to shut and keep shut the doors of industry against a class of people on account of their race, color and past condition. True, these organizations cannot easily be reached by law, although they are as much against public policy, order and government, as gambling, or as if they were to style themselves "An association for the purpose of hindering the spread of industry, and the degradation of a class." Such associations could receive no protection in law, yet such is the practice of what is called trades unions. These societies have not the claim to the respect or sympathy with which with some show the Knights of Labor might claim. Indeed, trades unions might well be looked upon as inciting just such resistance as Communism and Anarchism produce. But what is the true problem by which this social condition must be solved? As a moral inhibition, let our white brethren cease their hurtful discriminations based on color, in regard to the employment of labor in all departments, and remember that the best workman is the man of capacity and integrity; and that as two men of equal capacity can do more work than one, even though one is white and the other black, so can two dozen or two hundred of different colors of equal capacity. But the solution of this condition is also to be seen in its true politico-economical reason. It is well known by experience, that an industrious man or woman is an independent factor in the body politic of any community of people.

The Rev. Samuel Martin, in one of his Exeter Hall lectures, truthfully says the "man of industry is a better bred man. He is not a slave in creation, but a lord; he directs rather than performs; he never rejects aid; he creates nothing; he improves in every way his condition. So that the natural tendencies of industry are in effect elevation. Industry lifts the poor out of the dunghill and sets him among princes; it suffers not the head to drop upon the bosom; it allows not the eye to be downcast; hands that are under its influence never hang down. Industry is health. Industry is strength. Industry is wealth. When this opportunity is given to man," continues the author, "there are two tendencies developed—discovery and *invention*."

It is easy then to see the true cause why these great advantages are denied the Negro in the South, aye, and in many portions of the North, East and West. It is because his opponents well know that the Negro in his present condition is a dependent class, because he is a non-productive class; and that so long as he can be kept in this condition he can be controlled in all the various vocations of life, social, political, and often religiously. Then this problem is easy of theoretic solution, if not of practical adaptation, and is to be found in the colored people themselves. We first need *unity*, then action, in this direction. Let us commence in our schools and colleges to learn our youth the arts of industrious life. Let us, ourselves, by mutual help and mutual confidence, create for ourselves the opportunity for engaging in the industrious pursuits of life.

Colored men have been free long enough to conduct a loan and savings bank of their own. If, when a colored man desires to build a house, or have a new cart or buggy made, he would seek out his fellow colored citizen and employ him, he would do far more towards breaking down trades unions than a thousand resolutions or letters in the newspapers on the subject. And why? Because all trade and all profit depend upon the laws of reciprocity in profit. A man cannot long deny him whose service he needs in any respect his recognition; and, moreover, we must exercise this protection against an unjust prejudice which is exercised against us. So long as white people will discriminate, and, in spite of our competency, encourage their own only to learn trades, employ their own only in business pursuits, patronize their own color chiefly, wherein is the wrong for seven millions to be united against such a prejudice? It is thought by some that our numbers are too insignificant to be able to effect a reform. It may be so; but they are not too small to be able to afford protection, in that seven millions, abstracted from mutual and reciprocal benefit, as such, affects fourteen millions, if not more, in the aggregate.

Again, the social condition of the colored people of the South must receive a change from within themselves. They must seek to occupy position in life which will demand respect and recognition from the selfish standpoint of reciprocal benefit. There is now an endeavor among the laboring classes to leave the South and emigrate West in quest of better wages. The exodus from the South will be ineffectual in the first place unless the emigrant, wherever he goes, is capable of owning the soil. The idea on the part of white people of the South, that the Negro should not own the land, is a penny wise and pound foolish idea, as is seen in the labor troubles in Ireland today.

It is vastly better that a community of people should own lands in just proportion, if not in common, according to the idea of the political economist, Henry George, than that the lands should be possessed wholly by one class, or even in too large a proportion, and that another class should be forever tillers of the soil. This condition produces a class of dependents, who are tyrannized over and oppressed by the opposite class of independents. The unnatural relationship of man with his brother, is another cause of the social condition of the South between the blacks and whites, as seen in Courts of Justice, in the jury box, in the political arena, in domestic life and throughout in social conduct between the races. The laws of the South seek to preserve the social status of the whites, by prohibiting the intermarriage of whites and blacks. This will be effectual only as long as the condition of the two races is widely dissimilar. There is always an affinity for like elements to come together and dissimilar ones to repel each other. This is as true in social as in physical science.

But, to return to the need of change in the social condition which is to be brought about by the colored people themselves, I must repeat what I have said. This need is that of self-development in education among the colored people. We need an industrial education, because we need an education which teaches our youth not to despise work. We are in nowise socially advancing if our education teaches us how to despise certain classes of work. This instruction should be found in our colleges and universities whenever there is an industrial annex. This class of education must receive especial attention if the social condition of the colored people of the South is to be bettered. Not only should they receive liberal assistance from patriots and true philanthropists, but they must learn more and more to aid themselves. This can be done. The amount of money spent in the South among the colored people in supporting their churches and the vast amount of property of this character, which in the short space of twenty years they now own, prove conclusively their ability to elevate themselves from a more general industrial standpoint.

Some people entertain the opinion that, owing

to the small number of colored people in the United States as compared with the whites, they can do nothing of themselves. This is erroneous, and no greater proof exists of the capacity of the colored people to uplift themselves, in spite of superior numbers among the whites, than the fact that no other race on the face of the earth has been able to withstand the Caucasian, and not be well nigh annihilated, save the Negro. For thousands of years the Negro has been in the midst of the Caucasian, under despotic rule in government, if not in slavery; yet today he emerges stronger, more cultivated, more intelligent, wealthier and more industrious, than any other race under like circumstances. How is it with the Indian? Is he not well nigh exterminated under the white man's rule and by virtue of his contact? Has the Asiatic or Mongolian, alongside of the Caucasian, shown such improvement as the Negro? Slavery, from a social standpoint, has been regarded by some as a source of profit, from which through contact the Negro got his civilization. It may be, and yet it does not justify slavery. Its consequences show it to be the source of an evil social condition in the South, producing not only hostility between the two races, but a social misconfidence of the Negro in his own race. This is the chief reason why the Negro in the South has made no greater progress.

Poverty has also distinctly marked the social condition of the South, and although riches there do not now depend upon property in human flesh as it did in the times of slavery, yet its effect is the same today as before 1863. It has divided the South into what is known as aristocratic and plebeian classes. Between the whites the line of distinction is drawn between rich and poor; but between the rich whites and the blacks in general, the distinction is based simply on color, as no matter how wealthy a colored person may be in the South, his social status is but little improved thereby; and still it cannot be denied that a colored man of integrity and wealth secures some greater social recognition than his poorer brother. Money has the greatest magnetic power in allaying prejudice between man and his fellow. The social condition in the South, without regard to color, but as regards condition, is not due to bad crops only, as some allege.

It is well known that free labor has produced more cotton in the South than slave labor ever did, and yet one class of people, the consumer, is poorer today as a class—not a race—than before the war. The poor white and the Negro laborer find it impossible, as a class of laborers, to "get ahead" in the South at the present time. We must not look at the exception to prove this rule of statement. It is not because some of the laboring class have succeeded to accumulate a competency that this class is not suffering from an unjust relationship between capital and labor, as is most strikingly seen between production and the price of consumption. Just prior to 1861, and at the close of the war, cotton, the staple produce of the South, was nearly 300 per cent.

higher in price than today. In spite of short crops and because of East India competition, it is today 300 per cent. lower than at the close of the war. But what is most remarkable is, that the price of necessary consumption today is greater, when, by an increase of production, it ought to be much less.

Why is the cost of a yard of cloth today as dear, or dearer, than it was before the war, and this while the consumer before the war and at its close had twenty-five cents for every pound of cotton wherewith to buy his yard of cloth, and has now but seven or eight cents to do so with. This is the true cause of discontent and restlessness in the South today among the laboring classes, black and white. This difference is the true cause of the exodus, and not politics only. It is true that blind prejudice, the result of social distinction made by slavery, which causes one man to think his brother inferior to him because of color, manifests itself in lynching and wanton murders in the South. The true reason for this trouble is social disparity in condition, and not color, although the perpetrators of these cruel deeds themselves think it otherwise; in proportion to the knowledge of the true cause of this social difference, we shall find the colored man of the South emigrating from the South. Whether he will fly from the "devil he knows to the devil he doesn't know" remains to be seen.

It is also alleged that the Negro is shiftless, and this is the cause of his social condition in the South. How can it be expected of a people not versed in the science of political economy, and not allowed to come in such social contact with those who know of the benefits of a methodical thrift, to be as prosperous as those who do know these benefits? It would be well if every colored man in the South could learn this one truth, that if he cannot save enough from farming to maintain and support a family, he may provide for their future wants by insuring his own life through a rigid economy. Some say it does not benefit a man "to die to gain." It may not a man, but it certainly does a family. Suppose A has one son, and, amid the toils of farm life, he finds himself unable to save but $24 per year, it is easy to see how many years it would take to accumulate a decent sum which would materially benefit his son after his death. But suppose he had used this amount saved annually in paying his policy upon a premium of $1000, at his death his son would start into the world with an amount which would raise him above scorn and social ostracism among his white fellows of no greater worth at least. I recommend this among the things which we should do to enable us to lift ourselves to a social condition in the body politic of the South, nay, even in the North, East and West, but especially in the South, equally with our white brother. This financial worth is better calculated than anything else to change the American idea about the inferiority of the Negro race.

I have thus far ventured these views upon the social condition of the South and the causes and offered my humble suggestions of the true solution of this most difficult problem, as a result arising largely from my observation after ten years in this portion of our country and among its people. These views are not in anywise designed as a scientific dissertation on the social condition of the South, but only as observations and experience, arising in many cases from a practical knowledge. I believe the Southern white people tractable in the ways which will bring about harmony among the races. I cannot bring myself to believe that a people who are in present memory of the fidelity of the Negro towards them will much longer deprive him of his just rights and privileges, for "Just men only are free—all the rest are slaves." And truly the social condition of the South today makes all men slaves to their passions and to their prejudices, which bind them to the altar of stagnation like unto Prometheus to the rock, and the very vitals of their progress are being eaten out by their own prejudice.

But after all of these reflections and observations which I have made on this topic, its causes and effects, I have not only the hope, but the certain evidence, of rapid changes even in the social condition of the South. Capital, industry, morality, development, experience, contact, the extinguishment of old animosities, are all doing the work of producing a more harmonious condition among the two races. God speed the hour.

CHAPTER V.

THE NEGRO AS A CITIZEN.

In connection with the investigation of the New South I have deemed the following subject both relevant and pertinent. The question of citizenship in the South, as it was formerly in the North, is the subject of both controversy and diversity of opinion. I have deemed it therefore important to present my views on the Negro as a citizen and for the reasons following.

Among the ancient Greeks and Romans the civic capacity and the civil duties of every citizen were frequently brought before the public and the citizens were instructed therein. These subjects formed a part of the education of the youth, so that the value of citizenship became not a matter of indifference by the many, but pride in all; and no right was denied or privilege rejected a Roman citizen, but the invader was reminded by the proud exclamation, "I am a Roman citizen." The study of citizenship is incumbent on every American citizen, and ought to be a prominent lesson of instruction given in our schools to our youth. But more especially does it become the important duty of every colored citizen in the United States of every condition. And why? Because the doors of civil liberty have been closed against us for more than two hundred years and now are but partially opened.

Theoretically and in the light of the law we are American citizens; practically we are not. One hundred years have passed since our common country sprung from the unjust clasp of the Mother Country, held as a vassal, into the family of nations as a free and independent people. In this work of enfranchisement we assisted. The blood of Crispus Attucks, a Negro, was shed in behalf of American liberty and American independence. Then our citizenship is coeval with the birth of the great Republic. It is not a gift, but a right earned. Let us then enquire into what it means.

The word citizenship is derivative of the word citizen. A citizen, in the primitive and most comprehensive sense, means "one of the sovereign people," a constituent of society. At common law it means "an inhabitant of a city." This comprehensive meaning has for many years been combatted by a portion of the white race in America, so that in American law a citizen once meant "a white person born in the United States or a naturalized person born out of the same." This definition, to the shame of our country, was so generally accepted as true until it can even be found in our law books of olden times. The most comprehensive and true definition of citizenship is to be found in the opinion of Attorney-General Bates in the early case of the schooner Elizabeth and Margaret, of New Brunswick. This vessel was detained by the revenue cutter

"Tiger" at South Amboy, New Jersey, because commanded by a colored man, and so, by a person not considered then a citizen of the United States. The question propounded to the Attorney General by Captain Martin, of the "Tiger," was, "Are colored men citizens of the United States?" The answer given was worthy the head and heart of the man who uttered it at such a time, when obloquy, if not persecution, was the sure recompense. The Attorney-General's opinion was "That a citizen of the United States, without addition or qualification, means neither more nor less than a member of the nation. All such are practically and legally equal—the child in the cradle and its father in the Senate. *Prima facie*, said he, every person born in this country is a citizen, and he who denies it in individual cases assumes the burden of stating the exception to the general rule." This opinion, given many years ago, is now an accepted truth, a law. Thus it is that truth, crushed to earth, triumphs in course of time. For, in the language of Senator Sumner, writing in 1846 to Robert C. Winthrop, "Aloft on the throne of God, and not below in the footprints of a trampling multitude, are the sacred rules of right which no majorities can displace or overturn." Thank God, we are American citizens, and this fact cannot now be changed or the right deprived of us except by our own act in violation of law. Once a citizen, *natus* or *datus*, always a citizen, even to the uttermost parts of the earth; yes, in South Carolina as well as in Massachusetts or Michigan, and it should be protected everywhere with that fidelity which is due from government to subject.

Citizenship is derided and a mockery when any class or race cannot exercise its full privileges because of race or color. Crime may disqualify the exercise of the right of citizenship, but cannot annul or destroy it. Citizenship is of the earth—earthy. The Constitution of the United States, as it at present stands, with its amendments, declares "that *all* persons born or naturalized in the United States, and subject to the jurisdiction thereof, are citizens." The only division then of citizenship, as recognized by the Constitution, is the natural born and the naturalized citizen. There is no distinction then under the Constitution on account of color. It was in this view that the Hon. Charles Sumner, the friend of humanity, and the like of whom we shall not soon see again, whose name is the synonym for integrity, excellence of character, virtue, statesmanship, philanthropy, the colored man's advocate for his rights, the iconoclast of invidious distinctions under the law, between citizens, and the champion of equal rights for all citizens, introduced in Congress his famous Civil Rights bill, and although now made a practical nullity by our Supreme Court of the nation, yet lives in the hearts of a grateful people, and in the memories of seven millions of a once oppressed race. Wm. Summer, speaking of citizenship, and its rights and privileges as belonging to the colored man, says: "Ceasing to be a slave, the former victim has not only become a man but a citizen, admitted alike within the pale of humanity and within the pale of citizenship. As a man, he is entitled to all the rights of a man, and as a citizen he becomes a member of our common household, with equality as the prevailing law. No longer an African, but an American. No longer a slave, he is a component part of the Republic, owing to it patriotic allegiance in return for the protection of equal laws. By incorporation of the body politic he becomes a partner in that transcendent unity, so that there can be no injury to him without injury to all. Insult to him is insult to an American citizen. Dishonor to him is dishonor to the Republic itself. Whatever he may have been he is now the same as ourselves. Our rights are his rights, our privileges and immunities his great possessions. Not only is he a citizen, but there is no office in the Republic, from the lowest to the highest, executive, judicial or representative, which is closed against him." What burning words of immortal truth. Would to God fifty-three millions of our white fellow citizens believed today as Senator Sumner did. What peace, what harmony, what prosperity would attend our common country! And be it remembered, that Charles Sumner thus spoke as the exponent of the "Grand Old Party."

The political and civil equality of all men is derived from the origin of civil government. Men in their natural and individual state of existence, uncontrolled by human legislation, found in their wants and fears the necessity of organized society, which is called government, or as Sir William Blackstone says: "They discovered that the whole should protect all its parts, and that every part should pay obedience to the whole." It is in this light that our Constitution should be construed and our people dwell together. If this is true, then the idea that "this is a white man's government," when the white people do not comprise all of the American people, is a false and erroneous idea, one born in the prejudices of a race—not in the genius of our government. No one can fully discuss the citizenship of the Negro, without adverting to the various views which have been entertained in this country relating to his citizenship. The fact that it was a part of man's being, an inviolate right brought into the common brotherhood of man in the organization of society and government was discountenanced, and until the 14th Amendment to the Constitution was adopted, the question was: did not color or race deny the right of citizenship? But this has been always so. Man has always sought to deprive his brother of his civil rights by some force or subterfuge. It was so during the middle ages, until the rapacity and imbecility of John Lackland gave opportunity to the oppressed barons to wrench from him at Runnymede those civil rights, the bulwarks of English liberty—Magna Charta. "There is no part of the English Constitution," says Hallam, "so admirable as this equality of civil rights." It is precious to every man. It ought to be precious to us today. For more than two hundred years we have been denied of this right, governed without our consent. But now we are citizens. Nor are we new citizens, but citizens as old as the American Constitution, an essential part of the American body politic. We have need now but to understand what our rights of citizenship mean, then demand them; comprehend our duties, then perform them.

And now what are our rights as citizens? A right, in its most comprehensive sense, means "a well-founded claim." In law rights are divided into absolute and relative rights. The former are those which the American people in their Declaration of Independence said to be inalienable. They are the right of personal security, the right of personal liberty, and the right of private property; and these rights precede government. The citizen carries them into government with him. The right of personal security consists of a person's uninterrupted enjoyment of life, his body, his health, his reputation. Hence when a man is denied entering any public place, or is imprisoned without due process of law, he is denied a right of citizenship. The right of personal liberty consists in the power of locomotion, that is, moving one's person to wheresoever one's inclination may direct without interference, except restrained by due process of law. The right of private property consists in the free use of all we have acquired in the nature of property, real or personal, and to dispose of the same as we may choose, without control or diminution save by the law of the land. Now all of these rights belong to the citizen, and are only controlled by his suffrage or consent. It is easy to see then the great wrong done to a citizen to deprive him of his suffrage or his consent to control his absolute rights. It is robbery. It is political land piracy. It is still worse to deny him this on account of color or race.

Suffrage is the exercise of the privilege to vote, which is giving our voice, or manifesting our disposition by some symbol in the choice how we are to be governed. This is sometimes called a privilege in contradistinction from a naked right. This is correct. And yet the privilege of suffrage has been exercised by civilized governments for so long a time as to ripen into the right of the citizen. It is at least the undoubted right of every citizen of a free government, be it a Republic or otherwise. It was imperfectly exercised as early as the time of the Judges of Israel, when the people chose their rulers from the most brave. It is declared in the Scriptures "that all the elders of Israel came to Hebron and King David made a league with them in Hebron before the Lord, and they announced David King over Israel." In the days of Rehoboam the right of suffrage was more definitely exercised. When the people of Israel were about to elect a king they said unto Rehoboam, "If thou wilt be a servant unto this people this day and wilt serve them and answer them and speak good words to them, then they will be thy servants forever." In other words, we will elect thee our king.

The right to vote and give expression to one's consent to be governed is the foundation of free government. Hooker, the great divine and author of the history of ecclesiastical government, says that "All public requirement of what kind soever ariseth from the deliberate advice of men seeking their own good, and all other is mere tyranny." This right of the people to have a voice in the choice of their representatives is approved of God, who, when the children of Israel desired a king, spoke to Samuel, saying, "Hearken to the voice of the people." But the benefit of suffrage depends upon the right use of it. In selecting our rulers we should let honesty, integrity and proficiency be our guide, and not favor or money. Gather your leaders from such as Plato recommends. He says, "If one man be found incomparably to excel all others in the virtues that are beneficial to society, he ought to be advanced above all." It was the mistake of the Roman people that they allowed demagogues to be their rulers in civil life. Men who love office better than country are not fit to rule. Place good men to the front—white or black—for virtue has not her seat in the color of a man's skin, but in the purity of his soul. The idea of putting a man out of office because another wants it is one of the evils of our Government, and is detrimental to the public good. Indeed, a good representative can have no successor while living. The principles of government are not learned in a day nor the defects of government ascertained in a year, and yet the practice is too much indulged in and the error believed that we should change our rulers often. If a people cannot change their rulers when they would it only proves their inherent weakness.

The frequency with which the people of the United States change their rulers, is to my mind a detriment. It opens the door not only to political strife, but it also takes the industrious classes from their pursuits and leads them to the field of political battle, where enmities and bitterness of feeling arise. The diversity of political views change often our social relationship, and but little time is afforded for the cooling of political passions. We need to learn toleration in politics. It was this condition of political intoleration which I have referred to, that deprived this Republic in its early days of the most gifted and talented of our constitutional interpreters. It was the greed for office which led Aaron Burr to take the life of Alexander Hamilton. It consigned one to the grave of earth and the other to the sepulchre of oblivion in the just memory of a nation. And yet men should be jealous of the right of citizenship, and defend it even at the cost of their lives, when it is denied or any of its privileges abridged. Some think lightly of the ballot, and sell it or otherwise degrade the privilege, but it is the citizen's sword of defense. It is the poor man's protection, as well as the rich man's pride. Some say that the exercise of suffrage, which is the privilege of the ballot, should be qualified in its use for the good of society, and they propose, some a property qualification, others an educational qualification, and in this view it is held as the reason for the denial of the suffrage to thousands in the South, on the ground that the Negro is too ignorant to vote. I admit that ignorance is a foreign element in perfect government; but is ignorance marked by color? Is not government just as much jeopardized by the vote of the ignorant Frenchman, German, Swede or Irishman, as by the ignorant Negro? Why allow the ignorant foreigner to elect your President, and deny the right to a class of citizens born within the United States, whose only offense is a dark skin or a certain political creed?

The Negro citizen bought his ballot as he did his freedom—with his blood. Least of all other citizens, then, can he afford to stand silently by and see it denied him, or he himself disregard it. He earned it at Gettysburg, at Manasseh and at Port Hudson. When the question was put to the Negro soldier at Port Hudson, "Will you climb the ramparts and place the Union flag there?" the reply came fast and clear, "I will do so or I'll report to God the reason why," he there and then earned the ballot for his race, first registering that vote at the throne of the Eternal Captain of the human family. But I do not forget that thousands of our white brethren, did their share in this struggle for human rights. Their acts are registered in the City of the Dead at Gettysburg, where the immortal Lincoln once so truthfully said—speaking of the brave soldier who died that this Union may live undivided and indissoluble and we colored brethren live as free men and citizens—"The world will little note or long remember what we say here, but it will never forget what they did there"—pointing to the graves of ten thousand of our Union braves. American citizenship then, as possessed by the Negro, should be no bauble nor cheap commodity. And yet in the Southern States it is today a nullity in the possession of thousands of this class; it is a mere name without ornament or value. It finds no shelter in the American Constitution, no protection under its laws. It is left to work out its own destiny, either by compromise or subjection. But those who have denied us of the right of suffrage in the South will themselves first need it, for "He who teacheth bloody instructions, being taught, return to plague the inventor." No class will longer be deprived of rights than by intelligence, and power, they can demand them. The Southern vote cannot much longer be suppressed. The schoolhouse will be its emancipator, wealth and industry will be its protector, intelligence its guide, and courage and bravery its guardian.

Now, a word or two about the duties of citizens. Duty in its widest sense is analogous to right and is the higher degree of relationship between man and his fellow in government. Duty ought to be performed in obedience to a just conscience. It is defined to be "a human action which is conformable to the laws which require us to obey them." Duty differs from obligation, in that it cannot be enforced by law.

God has created within us a reason that we may understand our duties, follow the laws which regulate them, and perform them. Our duties are various and may be divided into natural and civil duties. It is our duty to eat and drink that we may live, to be temperate in order to preserve good health. It is no part of man's duty to so use intoxicating liquor that he cannot tell a corkscrew from a snake, and to so impair his health that he cannot perform the ends of life. Our civil duties are obligations resting upon us as members of society. Our civil obligations are expressed, our civil duties implied. The former arise from the contract entered upon by all citizens as members of the body politic, and these duties are as incumbent on us as are our individual obligations. When duly performed they tend to bind us together for the good of society and government. Men ought often to meet and find out their civil duties, as they go to church to learn their moral duties. Among the first of natural duties which the citizen need adhere for the good of society, is the maintenance of an education for his children. The first duty of a parent toward a child *is* maintenance. Puffendorf declares it to be "a principle of natural law, an obligation laid not only by Nature herself, but by the parent's own proper part in bringing them into the world; for they would be in the highest manner injurious to their issue if they only gave their children life that they might afterwards see them perish." In no manner does a parent perform a nobler act of civil duty than by a proper maintenance of his or her children. Some think that if they secure for their children food, shelter and fine clothes that they have completed their civil and parental duties. Not so. The training of a child means the securing of health and vigor to his body and the elements of high and exalted character in his mind. Character is the seed in a child of a noble and useful citizen. It is worth something to teach a child to test the character of his future acts in life by the question is it *right* judged by the eternal laws of God. I invoke such a training to such an end for all children.

The next duty is the education of the child. This is a most comprehensive word and means everything which tends to the proper development of the human mind. Education is the bulwark of a nation. Its diffusion is a national duty as well as an individual one. It will produce greater national prosperity than we now have, to secure the education of every American child in the nation. It will be the safety valve of the Republic in the time of danger. It will put a check upon anarchy and communism. The Prussian maxim is, "Whatsoever you would bequeath to a nation must be taught in its schools." This is seen in the early education of the American people. A pro-slavery education gave us pro-slavery legislators, judges, teachers and preachers. And even today our system of education in many parts of the country tends to divide instead of unite us. Our schools, in many places, by their operation, teach two races, distinct destinies and divided interests. Separate schools for distinct races have no right in a free government for the people, by the people, and of the people. They are the offspring of aristocracies and belong there. True citizenship means universal education for the rich and the poor, the black and white alike. Education is truly described, "A companion which no misfortune can depress, no crime can destroy, no enemy can alienate. At home a friend, abroad an introduction, in society an ornament." There is no greater lever by which the colored citizen can raise himself to the plane of full manhood, and in which condition he can secure the fullest recognition of his rights as a citizen, than by education. Educated brains are the best assets. Fortune may fly, rank and fame may disappear, but education lasts for life. It never fails. An educated mind can never be bankrupt.

This question as to who shall educate the citizen, is before our National council today in the shape of the "Blair bill" in Congress. It is the first and highest duty of the Nation to educate its citizens. We owe paramount allegiance to the American Government, and we should receive from it paramount protection; and there is no greater protection to the citizen than education. It is a safeguard for men and women, for be it remembered, women are citizens too. Some deny this right to woman, but if a citizen is one who is either born or naturalized within the country, by what process of reasoning can we reach the conclusion that a woman born within the United

States is not a citizen, except upon the theory of those interpreters of the Constitution, who say that the word "person" in the Constitution was not contemplated to mean a woman. This reasoning, you will remember, was the one used by those who denied the right of citizenship to the Negro for more than two centuries. It was fallacious then, and to hold to it in the light of events is foolish now. Indeed, man cannot much longer deny woman her political rights. She has wrenched from him her social rights and privileges—she will gain all others by her perseverance, her industry, her capacity. The right of citizenship, if given woman, is feared because the right of suffrage must follow, and most of us are terribly afraid to see women at the polls.

A man who is not going to the polls drunk, nor to fight nor steal, and is neatly clad and a gentleman, need not fear meeting a lady there any more than he would at church or in the market. The fundamental principle of our government, is the consent of the governed; how then shall we be just in controlling women's property, making laws which they are required to obey, and the violation of which we punish them for, and deny them participation in selecting their rulers. Law in its advancement, keeping pace as it has always done with the civilization of the age, has given to woman enlarged rights as to property—and property is the basis of the right to control in government. I advocate rights for women, because the rights of my race has been denied upon no better foundation, and "A fellow feeling makes us wondrous kind." But these views, as I entertain them, are not without modification as to married women, because the law recognizes the marriage relationship as a union of two in one. But to return to the topic of education.

The ignorance which pervades the masses in the Southern States, is appalling. It threatens the welfare of the Republic, and is therefore a proper subject for National regard. The devastations of civil war have rendered the Southern States incapable of bearing the burden of a thorough education of all its citizens, and even if they could, Congress should at least regulate and provide for the citizen as a right and duty from the government to its subjects. The education of the colored citizen is peculiarly the duty of the American Nation. It is a debt due him. Some say the colored citizen has not the capacity for mental development. Let me ask, is the ignorance of the Negro as lately emancipated one of inherent incapacity, or want of opportunity? In the face of 200 years enforced servitude, in which all opportunity to learn or acquire the knowledge of letters was denied, can any just one answer yes to this question? And yet in spite of this deprivation what is the evidence of our progress in education? In the short space of 25 years we have become school teachers, and educated preachers, lawyers, doctors, artists, journalists, authors, inventors and the like. But there is still another and higher view for the necessity of education for the masses beside individual benefit

—it is the effect it will have in harmonizing the two races. A superior and inferior condition in intelligence will always produce conflict. The strong will always oppress the weak. The school house only will produce this necessary harmony. It is there where the child first learns the universal brotherhood of man, as from the pulpit it learns the universal fatherhood of God. The playmate remembers with kindness his fellow schoolmate. his affection enters with him in business as well as in social life. But the fear arising here is the great bug-bear called social equality. This is a social myth. It is the mushroom whom fortune has thrown to the surface, or the parasite who lives on the social trunk of some great oak, who fears social equality because having no root of his own, he seeks to live upon other bodies. But education should be fostered because it strengthens and promotes the public welfare. It is to be observed that all nations who educate their citizens are among the strongest in power. Germany is an illustration of this truth. And what would Greece have been but for her schools of philosophy. But for the system of public instruction given by the philosophers of Greece and Rome the pages of history would not have recorded the learning of Aristuppus, Euclid, Alcibiades, Cimon and Pericles. I invoke a universal education for all the citizens of the Union, to the end of harmony, peace, love and union, so that like the Penticostal fire of old it may fuse together Parthians and Medes, the dwellers in Mesopotamia, Cretes and Arabians, Jews and Gentiles, black and white, into one undivided people. Let the great north whose schools are for the people, of the people and by the people, continue its bright example.

The next duty of citizenship is to obtain a means of livelihood, or, in other words, to be industrious. A lazy man or woman is a bane to society and is a bastard citizen. All labor that tends to supply man's wants, to increase man's happiness, to elevate man's nature, is honorable, and is a civil duty. None have a moral right to consume unless he produces. And this brings me to reflect upon the duty of the citizen to uphold and protect labor. Capital should aid, not oppress, labor. Our railroads, which spread over the land like a network, our steam cars, our magnificent houses, our fine equipages, our clothes, our paper, our pen, our cannon, our ships of war, and all our comforts and securities, are the result of labor—labor of the head and labor of the hands. The earth, the air, fire and water, God has given to man to secure his happiness by means of industry. A race of people has a standing among nations only in proportion to its education, morality and industry; and this comprises civilization. Men are enslaved in their rights just as long as they are unacquainted with them and the means of their elevation, viz: industry. Not even war is potent enough to enslave an industrious class of people. They may be conquered, reduced to poverty, their bodies may be kept in chains, but they cannot be enslaved. The Greek axiom is, or should be, the colored citizen's motto in his new sphere of civil life. Action! Action! Action! No people who have lived on the face of the earth and became civilized have ever elevated themselves to the standard of a high civilization resting upon their abstract rights. If the colored citizen desires to destroy proscription as practiced in the halls of legislation, in hotels and inns, first let them destroy their past condition. Law inaugurates right, but industry alone maintains and protects them and renders them permanent. The elevation of the colored citizen and his association with his white fellow citizens equally in the pursuits of industry, is the only true means of the future safety and prosperity of our country. Our composite nationality demands the equality of the whole of our citizens; for as the whole is made up of all its parts, so is the whole imperfect, unsafe, unsteady, without all of its parts. So that our white citizens fall short of their duty when they erect barriers against the colored man entering all the pursuits of industrious life, upon the ground of social distinctions. But colored citizens have their duties to perform to attain a position of civic social equality. They must first be united, next be industrious. They must be economical, if they would be independent. They must, above all, have race pride, and, like the German, the Irish and the French American, stand together and uplift one another. Find him among yourselves who can lay his hand upon his country's altar, served by no sinister purpose and swayed by no selfish motives, and when you have found him be true to him.

Our duties as citizens involve upon us responsibilities, since duty and obligation are reciprocal. As citizens, we have the burdens of responsibilities to share with others, and we have certain special ones, peculiar to ourselves as a distinct race of people. Our first responsibility is to fit ourselves for the high position of American citizenship. This must be done, as I have already said, by giving our sons and daughters a thorough education in all that tends to our elevation. A thorough education does not consist in the knowledge of books only, but in the art of living. This we need to know as a young race of people. In this, our first work is industry and economy. Let each strive for independence. Those of us who have elevated ourselves to a plane of independence among our fellows, are those who have learned the maxim, "Take care of the pennies, and the pounds will take care of themselves." Let us not be content to stand and wait, but move onward and upward. Let us strive to become masters of the soil. In olden times no man was denominated a freeman but an householder. Today no man is truly free unless he owns his own homestead. Let us strive to teach our young men and women trades as well as professions. We must engage in these industries alongside of our white brethren, for truly association begets assimilation. We must seek to enter all the avocations of industrious life. We must to this end learn the benefit of co-operation. What one cannot do of himself, let others join and do; and be faithful in our doings toward one another. A system of co-operative industries among the colored citizens would, to my mind, be productive of great benefit. Land associations, co-operative stores, loan associations, building associations, as well as literary associations, would tend not only to unite us, but to upbuild us as a race. Some people think they can best upbuild themselves either by pulling down others or by always holding on to the skirts or coat-tails of other people. Not so; let us seek to get the arm of our more fortunate white brother, and together move along in the work of life. Our best white friends are anxious to see us thus endeavor to rise. It is the crawling creature that mankind walks over unheeded.

Our chief responsibility is our elevation as a race. Many and strong are the obstacles which stand in our way; but they are not insurmountable. Let us only feel that we must rise by our own energy. Learn to help ourselves and others will help us. There are in America hundreds of men and women of the Anglo-Saxon race anxious to see the colored race elevated and are willing to help them. Already they have spent their money and their labor in our elevation. They have built school houses and paid school teachers for our instruction, erected churches and supported ministers for our moral elevation. For this we owe them our gratitude. Now we ask them to open the portals of industry to our sons and daughters, and let them share in the business of life with them and learn of them. We cannot pull them down, but they can uplift us. How can we secure this patronage? I answer, by fitting ourselves for the work. Have we anything to show for our fitness? Yes! No honest observer will deny that, in spite of the hindrances and obstructions put in our way through caste prejudice, we have made commendable progress in all the avocations of life. There is scarcely an industrious avocation in which the colored citizens have not forced their way and proven their capacity in proportion to the advantages given them. We have entered the professions and obtained the testimony of our sharpest critics as to our ability. There are artists, inventors, manufacturers, merchants and the like among the race; but these are the exceptions. The rule requires larger opportunity for us to become fully equipped. Unless this opportunity is given us, unless we can enter the counting house, the grocery, the dry goods store, the telephone office, the telegraph office, the printers' office, the factory, the engine house; unless we can guide the locomotive as well as fire the engine, unless we can place the brick as well as carry the hod, construct the house as well as rent it, administer the government as well as support it, our citizenship means nothing. It is but little more than a political bauble, a snare and a delusion. Let us then realize what citizenship means, what it calls for on our part, and what it entitles us to on the part of our government. My trust is strong that we will gain all these benefits in the near future. Let us deserve, then firmly demand our rights as citizens. Let us perform our duties without fear or favor. Let us recognize our obligations and perform them.

Citizenship and its consequent duties and obligations has, since possessed by the colored citizen, become the subject of great adverse criticism. Some have advocated one view and some another as to his capacity for advancement, until the unbelief in his capacity to progress and become the peer of his fellow white citizen, has been the *causa causans* of the many injustices heaped upon him, more or less, in all parts of the country. Men have vied with each other in the exercise of their talents and learning in endeavoring to show the Negro's incapacity for advancement in religion, morals or industry. The pen of hate has been dipped into liquid of a poisonous prejudice in order to prove how far below his white brothers he is. In this charge against us, 250 years of servitude and oppression have been left out of the premises and we are called upon in the short time of a quarter of a century to do the work of a civilization which another race has been a thousand years or more in achieving.

The colored citizen is denied his rights and privileges and the opportunity for advancement refused him to become industrious, and then he is called "thriftless," "ignorant" and "inferior." He is called upon to be the best of Christians, where no love is shown him or peace secured him. He is said to be uncultured and unfit for high social life, at the same time the doors of every avenue to social advancement are tightly closed against him. Is this just and fair? Is there no duty devolving upon our white brethren in this work of elevation of the race? Horace has truly said? "If you wish me to weep, you must first weep yourself;" and Carlyle adds: "If you would have others believe, you must first take the trouble to believe yourself." So, likewise, if our white friends expect us to do much in the way of elevation, they must do something for our elevation themselves. If you wish the Negro to be industrious, open the doors of your factories, your stores of merchandise, your counting house and other places of industry to him. If you wish him to be cultivated, drive him not from the contact of social manners; put him not in "Jim Crow" cars, as is done in the South; relegate him not to the rear in your theatres or churches or other places of social contact. If you would have him be honest, be honest yourselves towards him. Give him wages according to his merit, and not his color. This must all be done before the colored citizen can reach the high social, political, moral and industrial plane in life required of him by the hard taskmaster, who demands bricks without straw from the laborer.

There must be found among our white brethren men and women who can rise above their narrow prejudices, and remember that the color of a man's skin has no more to do with his character or his intellect, than the color of his hair or his eyes, and acknowledge, too, that however bad this lower stratum which is so much despised, degraded and oppressed, the vices have filtered down through the upper and middle strata through a period of two hundred years to the Negro.

When the demand is made for greater progress, be it remembered that God set apart forty years for the deliverance of the Jews from Egyptian bondage, and therefore our critics should not be so unreasonable, so unchristian, as to decry a race or think them unfit for high positions on earth or for God's kingdom in Heaven in a quarter of a century. If our citizenship and our advancement are to be justly measured these limitations should be granted us in the criticism made, whether in the North, South, East or West.

Is it not strange that those who complain, fail to see that Christianity has utterly failed, especially in the South, to make the white man and the Negro brethren. And why? Because the externals of Christianity are far better observed than its principles or its duties, so that men remember not as they should that "God has made of one blood all the nations upon the face of the earth." But when we take a retrospect of both races, and a careful observation of the present, we may yet justly exclaim with the poet:

> Fleecy locks and dark complexion
> Cannot forfeit Nature's claim ;
> Skins may differ, but affection
> Dwells (or should dwell) in white and black the same.

Every day is working out this grand truth. and we must hope on and hope ever!

CHAPTER VI.

PROTECTION VERSUS FREE TRADE.

The investigation of the new "New South" must be incomplete if the all absorbing topic of the present time in the United States is not in some measure referred to. The question whether the industries and productions of our country should, by a protective tariff, be guarded against foreign importations of a like kind which are brought into our markets for competition against those made or produced at home, or by free trade, is a vital question to the "New South." The two great political parties of the present day differ in their views on this question. The Democratic party declares in effect for free trade, which means an open and unrestricted commerce between foreign countries of their industries and productions, and those of our own made and produced at home.

Some Democrats give as a first reason for their advocacy of free trade that a high or even protective tariff was a war necessity, exercised for the purposes of revenue so as to revive our once depleted treasury. If this be true, is there no other and greater reason? Another reason is or should be, obedience to the law of self-preservation. I do not attempt in these brief views to engage in the discussion of a topic which the ablest minds of America and other countries have failed to satisfactory solve, but I do feel the necessity for calling the attention of the South, especially, to a careful deliberation of a question, which if answered by it erroneously, will do more to retard its hopeful progress than any other thing of which I can conceive. Some people say that a protective tariff is needed to protect our industries. This is true, but I say the greater need for a protective tariff is found in the protection it gives to labor and the laboring classes of our citizens. How it will affect the poor is of greater importance than how it will affect the rich. It is obvious even to the unlettered, that whatever lessens wages increases poverty. If free trade will so lessen the wages of the working classes as to make the hearth stone cold for want of fuel, the feet cold for want of stockings, the larder sparse because of less flour, the sick room occupied for want of medicine or the money to buy it, the school house empty for want of scholars, parents being unable to send their children to school, the homes cheerless for want of moderate luxury, such as the newspaper and other sources of knowledge, and all because to the wage-worker and to the farmer, articles of need for consumption are greater than the demand or ability to buy them. In such a case, free trade is a curse to this or any country similarly situated. Least of all sections of our country can the South court such a condition. Today its laboring classes feel their inability to stand under the oppression of low wages.

And why is this? Is it not because the present products of the South are subject to greater competition under the reduction of the tariff from what it did a quarter of a century ago under a higher tariff? But ten years ago cotton in South Carolina brought at the opening of the cotton market twelve, and sometimes thirteen cents per pound. Just after the war I am told it brought twenty, and sometimes twenty-five cents per pound. It now brings only eight and three-quarters to nine cents per pound at the highest. And why is this? Is it not because cotton is grown more in Europe and India today than it was twenty-five years ago, and because of cheap labor to produce it abroad, the demand is less and the price necessarily falls? How then can a Southern farmer be a free trader? How can a Southern Negro, comprising largely the cotton producing class, vote with a Free Trade Party if such a course will make his wages smaller, his rations less, and his home without food? But the Free Trader denies the above results and contends for greater prosperity because of less competition. He says free trade will help the farmer. Let us see. It is said that India wheat can be laid down in London at seventy cents per bushel and in New York, without duty, at seventy-five cents; with duty, at ninety-five cents; but, with the increased railway facilities, it is expected that the farmer of the East Indies will be able to place his wheat in New York at sixty cents per bushel. Now, if the present duty on wheat is not raised, what will become of the price of wheat in five years as produced in America? Let our farmers North and South answer. The lands in India are as rich and fertile as our own, and labor can be obtained from six to eight cents per day, without board, the laborer feeding himself. How then is it possible for our farmers to bring into competition their wheat with the foreign farmer's wheat untaxed? Now, these two illustrations bring the question of Free Trade and a protective tariff before our Northern and Southern farmers distinctly.

Now let us take a peep into the industrial department, where skilled labor and capital are needed. In 1860, under free trade, and in 1888, under a tariff, we find this difference: crockeryware is thirty-seven per cent. cheaper than it was in 1860; cotton goods are at least twenty-five per cent. less; and woolen goods, including dress goods and carpets, twenty-five per cent. less; silk goods, thirty-five per cent. cheaper. In 1861 our present protective system was inaugurated. Then the manufacture of steel rails in America was unknown. This industry commenced in 1867. Then we were paying for steel rails upwards of $150 per ton, including the duty of forty-five per cent. *ad valorem.* In 1870, a specific duty of $28 per ton was placed on English steel rails. In 1872, American steel rails were selling for $112 per ton, and in 1882, they sold for $39 per ton. How then doth it appear, as our Free Trade friends say, that a protective tariff increases prices of manufactures? If England could bring her steel rails to America now as she did in 1867, at $150 per ton, when would the South see in its poverty a steel rail along its road bed of railway? In no case has a protective tariff increased the price; to the contrary, it has forced the English manufacturer to reduce his price; and be it observed, that this reduction did not take place until our home competition came in and lowered prices, protected by the tariff.

It is said that free trade would enable the consumer to buy cheaper. Is this true, or is it a snare? Let us suppose that by free trade, every article made in England could be sold cheaper than our own? Would not this soon transfer all of our manufacturers to England, and pauperize our laboring class? Our manufactories would soon be asylums for the poor. But after all, the common sense of this question is found in our daily observations. If the protective system gives to the laborer less wages than the free trade system, why do our English cousins come so freely to American shores to seek higher wages for their labor? Why do they not stay at home? Does not the instinct of self-preservation teach them to go where labor is protected by higher wages? In the South, especially, I repeat, labor needs protection. If capital is needed for its development, if labor for its production, foreign imports cannot be allowed to be brought into an infant section in its embryonic state and paralyze it. It is said by the South that it needs capital for its advancement. It asks Northern and Western energy to bring their industries in its midst. Does the South require these things to be done under a system of free trade? Assuredly not. How long will the great industrial cities I have already mentioned, situated in the South, retain their present progress and prosperity, if all they manufacture should be brought into competition with like articles manufactured abroad?

It is said the question of free trade and protection has engaged the minds of the ablest statesmen of the past and present ages, and is yet unsolved. This would seem to make men of moderate opinions and intelligence shrink from the task, and yet are not questions once regarded as difficult, now easy in the light of advanced thought and new environments? Practical experience has done more to solve this question than learned debates. It is evident from experience and statistics that the United States has progressed greater under a protective tariff than under free trade in the past quarter of a century. This lesson of facts the "New South" must quickly learn if it would keep pace with the North, East and West.

I have offered these few brief remarks for the purpose only of calling for reflection in determining the question of tariff or free trade, what the "New South" needs for its advancement and prosperity. I have seen Southern stagnation and I now observe Southern uprising, and would have the plant in nowise blighted by foreign fertilization. I am the more anxious that labor should be protected, because I see near at hand a surplus of labor in spite of protection. This has already begun to produce anarchists, communists and the like order of men, who claim to be dissatisfied with inequality of wealth as produced by capital and labor. How great this dissatisfaction will grow remains to be seen. It is, however, evident that if by any means wages can be increased, this discontent will decrease. Will an overflowed market with the articles of consumption and the necessaries of life with no money to buy them do this? Let the Free Trader answer. Whether this country shall be a free trade or a protective tariff country is greater than any political party success. It is a question for every individual in seeking his self-preservation.

Free trade is offered as a remedy for a surplus revenue. Is not a surplus revenue as much the result of too much internal taxation, as it is the result of tariff on foreign importations? Both are the main sources of our revenue. Is it not wise to lessen domestic rather than foreign taxation? Are we to become richer by making ourselves poorer? Is not this a paradox? I am in favor of the reduction of internal taxation. The war is over and our need is less than twenty-five years ago. Our national debt is smaller and our country stronger, but we may easily, to my mind, retrograde to our place in 1861, if we allow our industries to be unprotected for the benefit of foreign countries.

Ex-Senator Benjamin Harrison, of Indiana, now the presidential candidate of the Republican party of the United States, said in a speech delivered before the Lincoln club, at Danville in 1886, in regard to the hue and cry of the Democratic party for a reduction of the revenue, "I want the reduction made so that the principle of the protection of American industry shall not be eliminated from our tariff laws. I want it made with a careful regard to the rights and interests of our own manufacturers, and especially to the rights and interests of that great body of working men, who fill the factories of our country." Now I don't think I shall go far out of the domain of this work to say, a President of the United States holding such views is a safe captain for our "ship of state." The poor laboring man can have no stronger friend in the views expressed above than Gen'l Harrison, who if elected to the Presidency of the United States, will place the interests of the country financially and industrially on a safe basis. Before closing this chapter it may be profitable to the reader, both North and South, to know what further opinion this Republican candidate for the Presidency of our great Nation in the ensuing political campaign, holds of the effect of free trade upon the South. His views are a warning to this section of our country, and if party political zeal should fail to prevail, will be be a blessing if heeded. Gen'l Benj. Harrison, speaking to the Commercial Travellers' Association of Chicago, Ill., and referring to the South, endorses the distinction which the writer has endeavored to make in regarding the South as a "New South." He says:

I am sure there is a "New South," shackled as it is by traditions and prejudices, that is girding itself to take part in the great industrial rivalry with England, which Mr. Spence so much deprecates. These great States will no longer allow either old England or New England to spin and weave their cotton, but will build mills in the very fields where the great staple is gathered. [Applause.] They will no longer leave Pennsylvania without an active rival in the production of iron. They surely will not, if they are at all mindful of their great need and their great opportunity, unite in this crusade against our protected industries.

Our interests no longer run upon sectional lines, and it cannot be good for any part of our country that Mr. Spence's vision in English trade with us should be realized. [Cries of "Never."] Commerce between the States is working mightily to efface all lingering estrangements between our people, and the appeal for the perpetuation of the American system of protection will, I am sure, soon find an answering response among the people of all the States. [Loud cheering.]

Should the "New South" take hold of free trade it must expect to see its present industries decay and die, its laboring population sink into poverty, its cotton manufactured and sold by European capitalists in its midst, in free and unfettered competition with native endeavor, and its whole territory another East India under the heel of European tyranny in commerce. The colored voter may well afford to lay aside all past wrongs and their remembrances for a period and save himself from the direful effects of lower wages, greater poverty, less education, and a condition, when brought down to a level of the laboring classes in Europe, little better than his past thraldom. This is what free trade will do for Negro labor in the South. And for the poor whites who are not capitalists it means the establishment of a peasantry class worse than in the time of the Romans, when Plebeian and Patrician, with all of their evil effects, divided the people and ruined the country.

CHAPTER VII.

THE NECESSITY FOR A BROADER AND HIGHER EDUCATION IN THE SOUTH.

Education, in its general meaning, relates to the development of the human mind and character. This in its effect is seen in peoples, states and nations as well as individuals. It is produced through circumstances, conditions and opportunities, and is general in its influence, thus distinguishing itself from knowledge as gained through instruction from books, and which is singular in its effects and influence. It is in the former sense that I speak of the education needed for the South, and not the latter, except in particular.

So vast have been the changes in the South in the past quarter of a century, in regard to its condition as related to its citizens and the institutions, commerical, political, social, literary and industrial, as to make any reflections thereon apropos in speaking of it. Let us first inquire what is the condition of the South and its need in relation to the composite nationality of its citizens, as divided into the two races—black and white. That there are in this respect conflicting influences and methods, which tend to sap and undermine the foundation of a sound social and civil progress in the South, is evident to the careful observer. Some have traced this condition to the late civil war, in which the two races in the South were arrayed against one another and in which the social and all other institutions of this portion of our country were greatly devastated or blotted out. This is too lamentably true to admit of denial, nor are we dealing with the past. Our question then is, What is needed to place the South—the New South, if you please—on a plane of commercial, social, political and industrial progress, like that of the North, East and Western portions of our country, so that our manufactories may increase, labor be protected, capital increased, and our inharmonious and dissimilar relationship as to the two races made harmonious and just.

Constitutions, wherein the fundamental rights of men as formed into society and government, have been quoted and applied, but have been found impotent to solve the problem. Disquisitions upon ethnological differences have shown themselves unprofitable and irrelevant. The narrow instruction which one class receives and which teaches only and always to serve and be contented with a station in life inferior to others, and which by its influence divides the people into an aristocratic and peasant class, and which was the education of the South during the dark days of slavery, will not solve the question. What then is needed? I answer a broader and higher education than that. One which enables its possessor to reach every station in life and to grasp the varied knowledge of mankind, past and present the world o'er, and be ready to engage in the advancement of the age in science, art, literature and industrial progress. Such would be a broader education than the South now possesses. One reaching higher and higher as it broadens. To reach this standard of education, the fullest opportunity must be given every citizen to prepare for the demands of the times, and to be ready for the spirit of the age. This is an age in which no individual, nor class of people can afford to stand and look on or look back, and if they do they must expect to be left behind in the march of progress. Like Lot's wife, they who look back, lingering with an eye on the past as some do in the South, will be caused to stand still as a monument of their folly. Truly says one: "This is an age of vast discoveries in science and in art. It is an age of ever-springing dogmas in church and state. It is an age of great development of mind and spirit of inquiry. Men are now no longer the recipients of stereotyped opinions or mere automata of some master's will or antiquated theory. Old axioms are rejected, established postulates are refused. Everything is in the crucible in this age, every theory is summoned to trial. No institution of the past can stand, until, subject to the searching analysis of the present, it answers to the spirit of liberty and freedom and marches to the tune of progress, law and equality." The South needs to learn all this and to mould and fashion its acts to the end of meeting these needs. The rapidity with which change follows change is remarkable. Events follow events, crisis comes crashing on crisis with so kindling succession that we no sooner look at one than we are astonished by another.

It then behooves us to look forward, and not backward, and to prepare for the future. A new aristocracy must arise in the South based on the genius of liberty, equality and progress. In all ages, whenever the education of the people was narrow, unequal in its privileges, recognizing a distinction among the masses, letters suffered and the progress of the people was small. This is seen in the suffering which great reformers endured in trying to broaden the education of the people in whose midst they live. It is said, "Petrarch and Dante wrote their illustrious poems in banishment; Ariosto and Tasso lived in want and died in despair; Cervantes, the author of 'Don Quixote,' could not command bread; Galileo saved his life by recanting; Locke was banished from Oxford; Milton sold his copyright of 'Paradise Lost' for £5, and 'Love Joy' was massacred." This all arose because the education of the masses was not broad enough nor high enough to meet the demands for reform and to enter upon the march of progress of ideas. It is not only capital the South needs, but it needs *broader ideas*, both in regard to government as well as the advancement of industry and the true progress of all its people. It must give free and unfettered opportunity for intellect to rise in whomsoever found, because if intellect is repressed in its energies, it will resist its oppressor and rise withal. The institutions of learning, which were once confined to the rich only, and which discriminated in regard to color, must obliterate their distinctions and must open their doors to all classes of citizens, so that where few drank before of the fountains of learning, thousands may now slake their thirst, since education and capital are the true needs of the South.

It is truly said that "the perpetuity of a nation does not depend on its resources, nor on the vastness of its territory, but upon the equal education of its masses." An equal education consists in the opportunity for learning enjoyed by black and white, the rich and the poor citizen alike. It also consists in knowing as well how to plant corn, to build a ship or house, to make a boot, as it does in translating Latin verse or solving a problem in mathematics. The South needs an education of its citizens such as will give strength, wealth, harmony and progress to every State. The benefits in an equal education are not only the diffusion of knowledge and the advancement of the citizen, but it also produces a higher degree of respect of citizens one towards the other, a unity and con-association productive of mutual strength. Nothing is so much needed in the South as a reunion of disintegrated classes of people in its midst. Nothing will sooner produce this than an education of its citizens broad enough for all of its citizens to grasp. Men of equal education and development of mind entertain equal respect one for the other, while a class divided unequally by education into what is known as the ignorant and learned, will always be in conflict, the intelligent, sometimes called the superior class, contemning and frequently oppressing the ignorant, or so-called inferior class. It is owing to the unequal advantages for education for all the citizens of the South, that so many differences arise. So then,

> "Let us pray that come it may,
> As come it will for a' that,
> That sense and worth o'er a' the earth
> May bear the gru and a' that;
> For a' that and a' that
> It's coming yet for a' that,
> That man to man the world o'er
> Shall brothers be for a' that."

A broader education is necessary in the South, so as to revolutionize old ideas into modern thought and action. There are some in the South who would still cling to the old methods as the ivy clings to the oak. They refuse to be educated in the new methods of agriculture, they reject the manifold implements and tools of modern production by which manual labor is reduced, they call the new methods of instruction in schools, "new fangled ideas." They revive the memories of the past when capital was in the hands of the few—and when industry was of an isolated character and "cotton only was king;" when invention as aids in manual labor was unknown or unthought of, because one class of people labored for another and not all for themselves, and when education was enjoyed by the few while the masses remained in ignorance. The idea that a broad enough education is needed so as to improve the condition of the citizen in the South is not yet fully entertained. There are some who are willing to improve their condition, while others are not. Above all other things an industrial education is needed in the South, because the natural tendencies of industry are elevation and independence. "Industry" says one, "lifts the poor out of the mire and seats him among princes. It suffers not the head to droop upon the bosom, it allows not the eye to be down-cast. Hands that are under its influences never hang down." Hence it is that a broad education is needed such as will give a strength of character to the citizen which books alone cannot give. It is the misfortune of many who are educated in books only to look down upon manual labor with contempt, and to regard it as belittleing. The past civilization of the South induced this belief. One source of wealth was relied upon, viz: cotton, and its patrons created an aristocracy, which regarded manual labor, as performed by the slave, as degrading. Resting upon the benefits of slave labor, no necessity arose for the development of industrial pursuits for the advancement of human progress. Now, in the changed condition of affairs, a new education is needed. It is one which teaches not to disregard industrial pursuits, nor to think it degrading to go behind the plow after leaving the college walls.

Signs of this new education are begun to be seen, and our young white men since the war have commendably commenced, after receiving a literary education, to engage personally in agricultural and other pursuits; not so with our colored youth. They rush into the professions, and avoid manual labor. The South needs a new industry for both races. It is an industry of the muscle, coupled with that of the brain. This need must be supplied in our schools, in which the pupil should be taught early how to dignify labor by knowledge, and how to make it profitable through wisdom. Thus we shall have a broader and higher education. That attention to this broader education in the South is already commenced, is evident from the establishment of agricultural colleges throughout the South. Now to these should be added our schools in technology, which should be opened to every citizen, rich or poor, black and white alike. This is not so at present. Even the sparse opportunity which there is to learn trades is narrowed and circumscribed in a large measure to one race of people only. The colored citizen cannot enter the work shop, the printing office, the engineer's shop, the telegraph office or merchant's store, except in the capacity of a menial laborer, because of his color. This narrow education of one class of the citizens of the South can be productive of no good, but will result in immeasurable harm. No place on the plane of the civilized globe has reached an exalted position in the march of progress upon such a basis, and the United States will not, for this obstruction is not attributable to the South only, but also to the North in a measure, which likewise discriminates against the colored citizen receiving industrial education. But we need especially this broad education in the South so as to make us a united people of united interests. Some people oppose the equal education of the two races, fearing it will bring about social equality. It seems rather to be the true apprehension that it will bring about equal ability. For what is social equality? It is the right which all persons have to regulate their family intercourse, the family being the unit of society. How then can an equal education of the two races affect these rights? It is a private right, and each person is the sole arbiter of such rights, and he who believes that "God hath made of one blood all nations upon the face of the earth," has all the guide needed between him and his fellow man. There is a difference between man and his fellow upon earth, as there is among angels and archangles in heaven, but it rests on merit and not color.

Indubitable evidence has the colored citizen of the South already given of *his* capacity for self-development, and in this he has added his share to the broadening of the education of the South, in that he has, by his advancement in letters and morality, taught the white man to lessen his prejudices against him. Not quite a quarter of a century has passed since this class of citizens of the South were in bondage, and denied all opportunity of engaging in the civilized influences of human life. Today thousands are educated and tens of thousands are receiving an education, not only through such assistance as is given them by the friends of education, but in a goodly measure through their own self-exertion. They have schools and colleges reared and supported by their own industry, and recently managed, controlled and taught by men and women of their own race. Has not all this had an influence upon the white man of the South? Undoubtedly so; and this is seen in the recent energies exercised by some white citizens in the South in establishing popular education. Distinctions, unfounded though they be, yet exist, but no one will deny that during the past ten years education has increased in the South. Our schools are more numerous, but our methods need broadening. Our country schools need more attention than is given them. They need better prepared teachers and greater facilities. A broad education of the whole people should be the foundation stone upon which the superstructure of the New South should be raised.

Equal education of the whole people will bring us closer together, and cause us to feel a common interest. It will put an end to unjust discrimination and prejudices, for there can be no difference between equals. If there is to be such a thing as one people in the South, it must be brought about by an assimilation of interests, by a common pursuit of a common end. But in this work of broadening our education, the duty rests not alone on the white citizen of the South, but on the colored citizen also. He must prepare himself for the future by his own energy; for "unless above himself he can erect himself, how poor a thing is man." Especially must this be the work of the colored man. He must have more self-existing force, and less reliance upon others. He must broaden his education so that it will reach all the avocations of life with his white fellow brethren, and where there is not a way to do so, make one for himself. If he cannot enter the avenues of industry entered by the white man, make his own. Build workshops, teach the art of printing to his youth, and all the mechanical arts attainable, establish his own places of business, and rely and have mutual confidence one upon the other, and the powerful force of competition in trade will soon break down all the barriers. "God helps those who first help themselves." Those who have done most are those who have chiefly relied on themselves. The only true development of a race is through itself, by itself. But this lecture is not addressed to the colored citizen of the South only, but to the whole South. We need a broader education than we now have, so that in every State, town, city, hamlet, or village the citizen can be instructed how to become a useful citizen.

The educational system of the South needs improvement. First, it needs to give equal facilities to all citizens to reach and attain the highest knowledge in every branch of learning, so as to meet the advancement of the age in which we live. New dogmas are arising, new theories are daily being propagated. The theories of Herbert Spencer, Kant, Muller and Tyndall, ought to be investigated by the colored as by the white pupil. Whether the doctrine of evolution, materialism or agnosticism are truths or fallacies, should be taught the colored youth as well as the white, because the development of the human mind should not be circumscribed. The greater the education of a people the more prosperous the country in which they live. Let the education of the South be broadened by beginning with needed reforms of old ideas in the school house, and extend them through every avenue along which knowledge is to be found, never losing sight of our industrial annex. Let the South open up public libraries, and schools of science and art, in which all can be instructed, and let her discontinue the penny-wise and pound-foolish policy of instructing only one part of her citizens, as if she were preparing rather for internecine strife, instead of equal improvement for all its citizens. Another profitable change in the system of education may be found in so enlarging the system by the introduction of what is known in England and her colonies, also in the North, as school inspectors, whose duty it is to visit schools throughout the counties and note their needs as well as their progress, and to find out the children who are not attending any school. Indeed, education is of so great need in the South among the poorer class of whites, and the lately emancipated race of people, that a law should be enacted in every Southern State, compelling every child between seven and fourteen to attend school at least four months in each year, or be subjected to confinement within the boundaries of some reform school—an institution most needed in all of the Southern States, not only for vagrants, but also for illiterates, and infant criminals; for it is the surest remedy against the spread of crime, to arrest the tendency in youth, and before habit becomes second nature.

But yet there is another reason for so extending the education of the youth of any state. It is this; every child who, if it lives, becomes a citizen, owes the state a reasonable service in the public school house as a measure of economy and against ignorance, pauperism and crime. A citizen needs to know the laws of his country, its commerce and its industries, in order to become a useful citizen. The colored citizen especially needs this broader education so as to be ready for the time when the the trumpet of knowledge in the hands of the enfranchised citizen shall throw down the now tottering walls of distinction, discrimination and caste prejudice. An education broad enough to include all the numerous branches of learning, and enjoyed by all the citizens in South Carolina as well as in Massachusetts will give to the South a government of an enduring foundation. It will transform darkness into light where ignorance prevails, weakness into strength, poverty into riches, hostility into friendship and discord into harmony and peace. But the South needs a broader education in the sense of possessing broader social ideas. By reason of its composite citizenship, the South needs to learn the necessity for unity and a common pursuit to a common end, namely, the uplifting of this portion of the country so lately devastated by the cruel fate of civil war, by all of its citizens alike. Discriminations and distinctions must give way to the broader spirit of equal and exact justice to all, without distinction of color or previous or present condition of servitude. The white and the black alike should enjoy the privileges of citizenship. A State which discriminates in the enjoyment of railroad, steamboat, or other public facilities between its citizens on account of color, is a State which needs a broader and higher moral education than it possesses. I know it will be said that the colored citizen must *deserve* before he can *demand*, and I recognize the truth of the proposition; but does he deserve being discriminated against on account of his color? Is all the education which he has received to count for naught, and the evidences of his material advancement to be disregarded in his right to enjoy equally the benefits of those laws which are enjoyed by his fellow white citizen.

The education of the masses is the great need of the "New South." But who shall do this stupendous work? Shall the States of the South alone do it? No one will doubt the duty of the State in this respect. Ignorance is the child of slavery which the South, although it did not originate it, yet nourished and sustained it, and ought to abide its consequences. This, many of the South have realized, and to their credit, be it said, that they are endeavoring to place knowledge within the grasp of every child. But we are citizens not only of the State, but of the Nation, and it is the prime duty of the Nation to educate its citizens as a measure of protection, and in the line of duty imposed by the Constitution, to promote the welfare of all its citizens. Education is not only the corner-stone of good government, but its safeguard.

There are men in the South who oppose taxation for the general education of the two classes of citizens, upon the ground that the white citizen, having generally more taxable property than the negro, is unjustly taxed for the latter's education. This is an erroneous premise and a false conclusion. Taxation of property is not for class benefit, but for the whole people. It is not unlike taxation for general protection. Can discrimination be made in this respect? Education is the common benefit of us all. It knows no section, nor party, nor creed, nor clan in its benefits. Each State, then, must do its share in the grand work. It is a social duty. It is also a moral duty, but above all it is an economical duty, because where ignorance exists crime and poverty prevail.

The South shows a larger percentage of crime than the North because ignorance is more widespread. It is therefore more economical for the South to build school houses than penitentiaries. Since 1876, and until now, the South has built large additions to her State prisons, while she has not built a single school house of reform for the many youthful criminals who are yearly sent to the penitentiary. An education which seeks to teach the State this necessity is needed for the South. In every State in the South there should be a school of reform. Nor is the law just which disfranchises an ignorant man for stealing a chicken, while the many public defaulters go scot free. Rather better put the youthful criminal in a school where he can be taught not only knowledge, but industry. But as I have before said, the duty of the education of the citizen rests not only upon the States in the South, but also upon the National Government. It owes us protection from the evils of ignorance. Let us see how great this ignorance which stares both State and Nation in the face. The illiteracy of minors from ten to fourteen years inclusive is said in the Southern States to be 448,146 whites, 541,410 colored, while in the Northern States it is 115,322 whites, and 8,088 colored, and in the Pacific States 15,726 whites and 3,273 colored. Again, in the Southern States, from fifteen to twenty years, the illiteracy rates, whites 263,404, and colored 803,826. Can this enormous record be said to be the duty of any single State to remove, or even of the Southern States collectively? Certainly not; but it is the paramount duty of the Nation.

The lamented President Garfield recognized this National duty when, in his first message to Congress, he said: "Next in importance to freedom and justice is education, without which neither justice nor freedom can be permanently maintained. The basis of free institutions is the intelligence and integrity of the citizen. This foundation is not simply indispensable to good government, but to the permanence and success of our Republic." Washington, in his Farewell Address, said: "In proportion as the structure of a government gives force to public opinion, it is essential that public opinion should be enlightened." Madison said: "It is universally admitted that a well instructed people alone can be a free people." What more do those want who hestitate about the duty of the National Government in regard to the education of all of its citizens? If the Southern States are not to be aided in the education of the citizen, then Congress should provide a National free school, wherein every citizen of the United States may avail himself of an education.

The census of 1860 showed in South Carolina 15,792 adult natives, not slaves, who could neither read nor write; in Georgia, 43,350; in Alabama, 37,302; in Mississippi, 15,136; in North Carolina, 74,877, and so on. This condition is much improved at the present time, but yet much remains to be done. The ignorance of the South is widespread, both among the poor whites and the blacks. To this condition may be truly attributed all of its drawbacks. It leads not only to crime—in lynch law and the like—but it perpetuates caste and social prejudice. It keeps divided the two races. A difference in condition always produces a discrimination, whether this difference be an intellectual or a financial one. But a broader education is needed in the South, not only in respect to the pupil, but also in regard to the teacher. Since Reconstruction, there has not been the highest regard paid to the qualification of the teacher, save in city schools. Many of our country teachers have been but little advanced over the pupil. Since the introduction of the State Normal Institutes, much of this condition has been removed, but the South needs more academies and Normal Schools, where persons intending to become teachers can be trained. But when these schools are established, shall there be any discrimination on account of color? First, to do so is to increase the expense of the State unnecessarily; second, it is without good reason. The citizens of the South cannot forever be kept separate, even though some may desire it. Education, and the advancement of the colored citizen financially and morally, are the surest destroyers of such distinction. These possessions have destroyed like distinctions in the North, East and West, and will they fail in the South. Can a reasonable, nay a sensible white person, have any well-founded objection to sitting under the same roof, or upon the same bench, with a well-dressed, well-behaved colored person in a training school, any more than he can to sit in a jury box, or, as in many places, in a railroad or street car? Indeed, does the South expect to receive National aid for education, and then discriminate in the education of its citizens on account of color? Had the South not better think over these discriminations and prepare itself to receive a broader education of the rights of the citizen? Make distinctions if you will; they are sometimes necessary, but do not base them on color. Fitness is the only true test.

If the South will adopt, as I think it must, and is gradually doing, these broad ideas as the true need of its development, namely, the equal education of all its citizens and the universal opportunity for industrial advancement of all, the hum of the spinning wheel and the sound of the manufactory's whistle will ring in her ears, railroads will cover her land as a spider's web, the ring of the anvil will follow the church bell, and we will soon rejoice in a "common brotherhood of man" as well and as fully as we acknowledge the common "Fatherhood of God." Mr. George W. Cable has truly said: "There is no distinction *per se*—it is caused by condition, and through condition must disappear. Education chiefly will produce this new condition in which social distinctions will disappear." Senator Blair is reported, in his address delivered to the colored people at their Fair in Raleigh, N. C., in 1886, to have said to them: "Get education, get land; get the best of both. These are the only levers by which you can ever hope to elevate yourselves. The refinement which comes with education will make you respectable in your own estimation." This is very doubtful language, but, coming from such a source, does not admit of any intention to do the colored citizen a wrong. Nevertheless, we will say that education will certainly make the Negro respectable in the estimation of the just. But some people in the South object to a broad and high education for the Negro on the ground that it will obstruct labor, and the question is asked, if the Negro is educated what will become of our fields? This alone is enough to show the necessity for a broader education for those in the South who entertain such narrow ideas. The good and beneficial effects which universal education produces on all classes of citizens is seen in Germany, in which country the farmer is educated, the soldier is educated, the politician is educated, the poor is educated as well as the rich; so that when William of Prussia met the Austrian army with his two and a half per cent. only of illiterates, against Austria's seven per cent. of uneducated, there was no doubt in the mind of those who well knew the power of an educated army, about the victory at Sadowa. "No system of public education is worth the name unless it creates a *great educational ladder*, with one end in the gutter and the other among the stars," etc. Behold the breadth and height of this education! A noble structure, with a platform at the bottom upon which all classes can stand. This is the education the South needs. Such an one will burn up to ashes old ideas, and out of the ruins erect a broader and higher education, directing its citizens by a strong and steady light to the safety, honor and welfare of our common country, so that we may, in the strength of our unity,

> Bid harbors open, public ways extend,
> Bid temples worthier of God ascend.

This work is in the hands of both races. What is most needed is courage, manhood, independence and perseverance. Our white fellow citizens need learn not to look upon the colored citizens who have grown up in their midst, in their families, and around their hearthstones, as aliens and foes, but citizens of a common country and entitled equally to the rights accorded the Irishman.

Frenchman, the German, the Swede, the Russian, the Italian and the Greek, and all others who form our composite nationality. These are but one great national chain, which binds the States together — strike out one link and you render the chain weak.

In my plea for a broader education for the South, so that its masses may be elevated, I am emboldened in the prospect for such new ideas as will produce a new relationship, even in its political dispensation. Although many doubt and fear the future of the Negro in the new political era, I have none. Reforms never go backwards, and I feel that every political party in power, be it Democratic, Labor Party, Independent or Prohibition, must take up the Negro where it finds him, and from the state the Re-Republican party brought him, and carry him further on in advancement and elevation. It is true that the past history of the Democratic party's treatment of the Negro in his rights, political or social, is no guarantee for the future towards the Negro, unless it accords him his rights as a citizen. I believe a friendlier feeling will yet dawn upon the two races in the South.

There is a strong disposition arising among the whites to recognize the common interest between himself and his "brother in black," and this, though slowly, is certainly increasing as the education of the masses broaden. Let us then trust that, like the Pentecostal fire of old, the new education arising among the two races in the South, may so act that it may fuse them like of old—Parthians and Medes, dwellers in Mesopotamia, Cretes and Arabians, Jews and Gentiles, black and white—into one undivided whole, so that the antagonisms of race, the hatreds of creeds, the rivalries of business, the prejudices of caste and the denials of rights might disappear, and the pure gold of brotherly love appear amidst the enjoyment of a broad education, as broad as the human knowledge and as extensive as our common country, so that soon will that period appear which Senator Sumner, looking down the vista of time, saw coming. Senator Sumner lived when the bud of political reforms had scarcely unfolded its petals; yet his scrutinizing eye of statesmanship saw the beautiful flower now unfolding in the harmony between North and South, and the growing recognition of the black race. He saw all this when he advocated the abolition of all the names of victories obtained by the Federal over the Confederate armies, as they may appear on the regimental colors of the United States. In his speech in Congress he said, "There should be not a union of conquerors and conquered, but a union which is the mother of all, equally tender to all, knowing of nothing but equality, peace and love among her children." "Do you want," said he, "shining mementos of your victories? They are written upon the dusky brow of every freeman who was once a slave; they are written upon the gate-posts of a restored union, and the most splendid of all will be written on the face of a contented people, reunited in common, national pride." How best can this prophecy be fulfilled in the South? I answer, chiefly by the education of the masses, not only in letters, but in the knowledge of a true unity and community of interests of all citizens without regard to color, so that we might be ready to meet the ever-changing times, and the fearful crisis which threatens our social government, as in Russia. Nihilism is within our borders, as was seen in the fearful tragedy of Guiteau, enacted upon our late lamented president, James A. Garfield.

Communism is at our doors, and is seen stalking almost daily in the marts of business and trade bearing the inscription, "Labor *versus* Capital." Dynamite lurks like an insidious serpent in our homes and official circles. The laborer no longer crouches at the door of the rich capitalist, asking for just wages, nor is content with a modern kind of feudal tenureship in land, keeping him always ready to serve his liege lord; but rather demands by co-operation, justice and equality in the means of a livelihood. The South cannot escape these crises; they are incident to every new development, every unequal growth in prosperity and opportunity. If, then, these disturbances are to be avoided, we must first educate the masses, next protect labor. The American mind is one in the developments of cardinal ideas. Until an idea is developed in the minds of the American people, it is useless to force it; but it can be educated. It was the idea of equality of rights that gave birth to American independence. The education of the South must be one which will give life to the idea of the necessity for justice to labor. This will enhance the prosperity of the country, and tend to the establishing of a "New South," whose superstructure shall rest upon right and a high civilization. Justice, equal rights before the law, and brotherly love, shall be its pillars; its corner stone shall be christianity; morality, the ornament of its walls; industry and capital its strength; education, its life; manhood and truth, its glory for ever.

In the broader education which I have described is included a higher one. As the South advances in material growth, as her resources are more and more developed, her sons and daughters need have the highest education attainable commensurate with its development. Science must be taught that it may be applied to her mineral resources and to the production of inventions. The pupil must not be restricted in the topics of knowledge, but must be educated in all the branches of science and of art. The laws of political economy must be well understood by the citizen, to the end of learning how to secure the greatest production from a wise investment and to regulate the just relationship between capital and labor.

In the development of the South, this branch of education should be taught. But above all, the education most needed in the South is the training of teachers in the art of teaching. It has been well said, that the art of teaching is a profession. It is one of the highest of professions, and anciently was held not by pedagogues, but philosophers. Socrates, Plato and Aristotle were school teachers of the highest order, and the world today is indebted for the wisdom they taught. What would Greece have been but for her schools of philosophy, art and logic. But for this system of public instruction in the higher branches by these ancient philosophers to the youth of Greece, the pages of history would not have been adorned by the learning of Aristippus, Euclid, Alcibiades, Cimon and Pericles. These men gave prestige to Greece and caused her to be acknowledged as the seat of learning in her times. She rocked in the cradle of her schools the wisest men of the world. It is even so with modern countries of renown. The South, with its great possibilities, must give to her citizens the highest possible education. Indeed, the spirit for the spread of education and the work of giving to the pupil the highest education, must extend as the rays of the sun upon the earth, and like it must vivify all upon whom it falls, giving strength to the teacher and beauty to the pupil.

Like as the sun sheds its light upon the flowers of the garden, developing their beauty, fragrance, and gorgeousness of color, upon all alike, so, likewise, must a broad and higher education in the South shed its influence upon all its citizens, developing a moral and intellectual growth and beauty, and by their influence give beauty, integrity and wealth to the great South-land.

CHAPTER VIII.

CAPITAL AND LABOR; AND THE TRUE RELATION OF THE COLORED CITIZEN TO LABOR ORGANIZATIONS IN AMERICA.

In introducing these subjects for consideration, I intend in nowise to attempt their scientific meaning; but only to ask consideration of them, as they present themselves to my daily observation and experience.

Capital and labor, and their relation to each other, and the duties and obligations arising from their representatives, are topics which have greatly agitated the minds of the American public for many years, but of late they have grown to such momentous proportions and importance, as to call for National interference. It therefore behooves every citizen, North and South, to make himself acquainted with these topics, and the causes of difference which arise through different views held towards them. The great irritation which has arisen between the representatives of capital and labor, which is manifested in strikes, labor organizations, and even attempted anarchy, is worthy of consideration. It is evident from recent events, that the inharmonious condition existing between capital and labor, threatens the very life of our government, and retards its true progress. The disproportion between capital and labor in this country, as in foreign countries also, is seen in the great moneyed corporations and individual wealth on the one hand, and the struggling laborer and low wages on the other. No one can escape observing how some men have become immensely rich; adding to their wealth in fabulous sums hourly, and by reason of their riches have the power to oppress the source of all riches, namely, *labor*, and thus create an unjust competition in the means of making a living between two classes— the laborer and the capitalist. The moneyed corporations, as represented in railroad organizations and large manufactories, give to our country what are called our "railroad kings;" and the low wages which the laborer receives in producing these riches have produced such a disparity between the two classes, as to call for the consideration of both—the cause and the remedy. We all know that these two forces (labor and capital) in the social development of man, ought not to be in conflict. There is no just reason why so many men should be poor and in want, unable to comfortably provide themselves with homes, and give a suitable education to their children, while others possess more money than they well know how to use, and yet refuse to alleviate the sufferings of their fellow man or promote his happiness. Some people who are wealthy think that if when they die they bestow some charity upon their fellow man, that they have performed their whole duty while living.

In this country, and under the genius of its

Constitution, it is no small concern to observe how wide one class of its people is becoming apart from the other; how hostile their aims and purposes in life, and how little they know of each other, because of social distinctions made so markedly by wealth, as it separates itself from poverty. Some men are the owners of thousands of acres of land and countless mansions, while others are without a spot to lay their head. Does it not seem that this unequal possession of this world's goods is at variance with the will of Him who is no respecter of persons? Someone has truly said, "The earth is a vast magazine of materials, and man is an artizan placed in the midst of these stores to discover their uses, and to appropriate them." It then follows that the source of wealth being common to us all, nothing is required but opportunity. Let us then examine these two great forces in the economy of man's destiny and fortune, and find out, if we can, why they are in discord; for as Henry Ward Beecher, speaking of capital and labor, has truly said, "They are one under a new form. The capitalist is the laborer under circumstances, and when the laborer earns *his* dollar, he is a capitalist to all intents and purposes." This view of the relationship between capital and labor shows the great reason why there should not be such envy, hate, and injustice between the representatives of these two great forces, and why protection to labor from home oppression, as well as foreign monopoly, should be demanded. Now, what is capital? To this question several answers may be made, as given by the lexicographer, the politico-scientist, and thorough experience and observation. Worcester defines capital as "The stock invested in any business, company, or institution."

Amasa Walker, in his "Science of Wealth," defines capital as the "Labor of the past;" in other words, "accumulated labor." He says, "Labor enters into production, or the creation of values in two ways. First, as labor of the present; second, as labor of the past. In their nature they are identical. They have assumed different forms, and have acquired independent rights. * * In practice, the two forms of labor must come together and help each other, if they would effect the barest subsistence of mankind. As society goes forward to plenty, comfort, luxury, and civilization, the union and mutuality of the two become more intimate and vital." Of the relation of capital to labor he says, "They are not antagonistic. All their effort, even in the severest assertion of their individual claims, goes to the increase of the common property, and the advancement of their mutual service. Antagonism tends to destroy. This is its purpose, so far as it proceeds to remove one or the other of the parties. * * * They are partners, and should divide the results of industry in good faith and good feeling. * * * Capitalists may encroach on labor. Laborers may, in their madness, destroy capital. Such is the work of ignorance and evil passions. However far such a strife may be carried, it must result in mutual injuries.

* * * The condition of well-being is peace." These are the views of one of America's foremost scholars in political economy, in which the theory of the science of the relation of capital to labor is most happily epitomized, but the practical proof of the truth of this theory is before our eyes daily. It is with this question that Henry George deals, and while I do not endorse his entire theory, I yet admit that he has done much in his writings to dispel the false illusion which led to the belief that capital is and should be king over labor.

Henry George, if I understand him correctly, would place all property in common, as being in accordance with God's original plan for man's possession of the earth. This lacks the power of practicability. It nevertheless is apparent that this world's goods are too unevenly possessed to secure that peace and happiness, which Mr. Amasa Walker declares ought to be promoted by the union of capital and labor. We cast our eyes around us everywhere in this broad land, and we see as between what is called capital and labor, the truth of the lines of Mrs. Sigourney, "Ye build! ye build, but ye enter not in." This is the laborer's complaint today in America, his burden in Europe. We find one portion of mankind lordly owners of extensive manors, enjoying ease and luxury, produced by the untiring labor of his fellow man, who at the same time is eking out an existence. It matters not what scientists or political economists say about supply and demand, and about the production of capital—that wages are drawn from capital and the like, the question still presents itself, and like Banquo's ghost, will not down. "Why, in spite of increase in productive power, (which is capital in stock) do wages tend to such a minimum as will give but a bare living? Go to New York, or any of the great cities of the North, East and West and behold the extent of capital, which is labor's produce, as seen in the mammoth stores, the countless millions represented in railroad corporations, steamboat companies, manufactories and the like, as owned by a few men, who in comparison to the population around them, are like a grain of sand to the whole sea shore, and then go into the dens and slums of the alleys in these cities and see the poverty, the incomparability between the denizens of these alleys and the capitalist, Jay Gould. Oh, says the moralist, this is the want of thrift and industry; but there is yet another class whose condition is equally bad. I mean the industrious artizan, as well as the mere manual laborer, who toils from sunrise to sunset, and who has to bear the responsibilities of life equally with his rich brother. He has to pay taxes, he has to support a family, provide for their comfort and their education and to fit them for future life, and yet is unable to do so because of low wages, or in other words, through the inequitable relationship between capital and labor. The laborer looks upon the railroads which he has constructed, or the ships which he has built; he sees the numerous articles which by his labor he has produced, and which serve to enrich the employer, while he remains poor, and he asks himself the question, why is it thus? Why, "for the few, broad lands and gold. For the many, starvation and six-feet-two of charity mould."

Capital not only oppresses labor by inadequate wages, but by the greater injustice of requiring too much time for the wages paid. Of the twenty-four hours in a day some men are found toiling for eighteen hours, thus destroying their physical development and their mental growth. The laboring classes are poor, because by low wages they are reduced to poverty. In Tyrol, it is said, first-class cocoon winders receive for seventy-two hours' work $1.80, and then are employed only at certain seasons. They pay for lodging and boarding forty-five cents per week; their food, of course, is cornmeal cooked with salt and water and a little salad or salt fish. This is the condition of labor in Spain in producing the most lucrative article of commerce there. How like this will be the poor laborer of this country if free trade is introduced in our land? In the South labor is chiefly in the production of cotton, the staple produce of the South, which made this portion of the country before the war the richest, and since freedom, the only source of the capitalist's most profitable investment. And what are the wages of the farm hand in the South? Not more than fifty cents per day, out of which he must eat and clothe and shelter himself and family. I plead, then, for a more equitable treatment of capital to labor, so that an honest laborer may find the means of living comfortably. It is sometimes urged that the reason for this inequality is that the man of intelligence and industry will always secure wealth, while the ignorant is poor and will remain so. Is this generally true? Is not the very intelligence of the laborer which refuses to brook the oppression of the capitalist the reason? This error of belief must change. The times demand it. Justice demands it. The safety of the country demands it. Labor depreciated and oppressed affects not only individuals and communities, as they are divided into classes of people, but it affects the purity of a government.

The outstretched, massive arm with which capital overawes labor, has sent into our law-making bodies a tide of corruption, which, in its flow, carries the poor man into the position of a political serf. The laborer, knowing how impotent he is to resist capital, because he is poor, is frequently the tool of the capitalist. His will is scarce his own, his judgment is made according to another's direction, and not the result of his conviction, and his choice is subservient to selfish interests and not his country's good; hence we find men elected to office who are in nowise the representatives of the people, but of some moneyed corporation. He is not a friend to the poor, because he has never felt his wants; he knows nothing about labor of the hand, and frequently of the brains either. He forgets that whatsoever he possesses, whether by inheritance or through his present wealth, is the production primarily of labor—labor of the head or of the hand, or of both, as they are seldom separable. Is labor then inferior to capital, since production lies at the basis of all progress? No. I am therefore in sympathy with any organization whose aim is to *reform*, not *destroy*, capital. I urge on to no strife, but there is an evil, a great wrong in some men being so rich as to keep others necessarily poor. I say to oppressed labor, *strike* on, not by mobs and bombs, but through organizations dedicated to reform—reform in which the work will be not *destruction*, but *construction*. Old customs must be pulled down, and new principles reared up. The object of labor organizations should be to strike the fetters from the mangled form of poor, prostrate labor, now lying at the feet of capital. Capital in its present condition is aristocratic, and drives mankind into dual parts—the lord and the vassal. It enters even into the courts of justice sometimes, and frequently shapes the laws of the land. In the administration of justice it sends the poor wretch for stealing a chicken or some corn to the penitentiary, but for filching the public purse, or defaulting as treasurer, the culprit usually goes free. Murder committed by a poor man is defined "the killing of a human being with malice aforethought;" but when committed by a wealthy man it is *insanity*, or self-defense. It is the voice of capital that makes back seats for Negroes in churches and theatres, and provides a Jim-Crow car for colored ladies and gentlemen on the railroad, and refuses them admittance into public places of accommodation in our South land. It is the iron hand of capital that does all this, turn and twist it as you may. And why this? Has labor no rights which capital is bound to respect? Let us see. What is labor? In the general acceptance of the term labor is the law of the Universe, and in a secondary sense it is the law of humanity; hence labor cannot be circumscribed within the limits of manual labor only, but is the exercise of genius and skill as exemplified more clearly in what is known as industry —for instance, the capitalist who is the merchant, is a laborer in his business; the lawyer who frames a deed or mortgage, or draws a will; the physician who prescribes medicine or amputates a leg; the historian who deduces from the experiences of the past, directions for the present and hopes for the future; the philosopher, pondering the deep mysteries of being; the man of science, hammering from the rocks of the earth the long buried secrets of her past existence, weighing the sun, measuring the sky, foretelling the motions of the planets and calculating the distances of the stars; the painter and the sculptor, making the rude marble breathe with life, and the canvass glow with feeling; nay, even the orator, in his utterance of noble thoughts as lawyer, preacher, lecturer—all these are laborers, and must be included when we speak generally of the rights of the laborer.

There is mutual relationship between labor and capital, hence Amasa Walker most beautifully describes this relationship when he says: "The union of capital and labor will be most effective when each is sure of its just reward. If the rights of a man as a holder of property are sacred, and his rights as laborer equally so, the greatest motive to production can be secured. * * * There cannot come out of earth, or heaven, a blow that levels all industry in the dust so quickly and hopelessly, as wrong done between labor and capital. Pestilence, drouth or floods do not so thoroughly and permanently prostrate the strength and hopes of a country as a breath of suspicion on the union of the two great agents of production. * * * If foul play or legal fraud comes between labor and capital and their reward, the very life of industry ceases. * * * The spring of work is broken. Labor suffers. Capital has the privilege of Leviathan," and we may add, it never fails to exercise it; but says Mr. Walker, "If labor goes under it, capital dies. The union of labor and capital is most effective when the latter is appropriately distributed. Capital creates no value by its own powers. It must be joined with labor. Somebody must use it, bring his personal energies to bear upon it, set it in motion, watch its operations, work with it." What truths! They ought to burn and consume the obtuse consciences of those capitalists who seek to oppress labor by an unjust and inadequate compensation in wages. It ought to put to shame the employer, who in order to keep his feet upon the neck of the honest Negro laborer, pays him as in the South, in tickets instead of cash, and makes him pay fifty per cent. for his rations; who puts rents so high, and pays so little for his cotton, as to make the poor farmer forever toil on, and toil ever, without being ever able to save a dollar.

So likewise with the foreign capitalists who pay feeble woman twelve cents a dozen for making shirts, and the factory hand $2 per week for a days' labor of sixteen and sometimes seventeen hours. What does labor for man's comfort and happiness? It clears the forest and drains the morass, and makes the wilderness rejoice and blossom as the rose. Labor drives the plow and scatters the seed, and reaps the harvest, and grinds the corn, and converts it into bread—the staff of life. Labor, tending the pastures and sweeping the waters, as well as cultivating the soil, provides with daily sustenance the millions of men, and women, and children upon the face of the globe. Labor gathers the gossamer web of the caterpillar, the cotton from the field, and the fleece from the flock, and weaves it into raiment soft, and warm, and beautiful—the purple robe of the prince and the gray gown of the peasant being alike its handiwork. Labor moulds the brick, and splits the slate, and quarries the stone, and shapes the column, and rears not only the humble cottage but the gorgeous palace, and the tapering spire, and the stately dome. Labor dives deep into the solid earth and brings up its long hidden stores of coal to feed ten thousand furnaces, and in millions of habitations to defy the winter's cold. Labor explores the rich veins of deeply buried rocks, extracting the gold, the silver, the copper and the tin. Labor smelts the iron and moulds it into a thousand shapes for use and ornament, from the massive pillar to the tiniest needle, from the ponderous anchor to the wire gauze, from the mighty flying wheel of the steam engine to the glittering bead. Labor hews down the gnarled oak and shapes the timber, and builds the ships, and guides it over the deep, plunging through the billows and wrestling with the tempest to bear to our shores the produce of every clime. * * * Labor, possessing a secret far more important than the philosopher's stone, transmutes the most worthless substance into the most precious. Labor * * * spans majestic rivers, carries viaducts over marshy swamps, suspends aerial bridges above deep ravines, pierces the solid mountain with its dark, undeviating tunnel, blasting rocks and filling hollows. * * Labor draws forth its delicate iron thread, and stretching it from city to city * * * through mountains and beneath the sea, realizes more than fancy ever fabled. It constructs a chariot on which speech may outstrip the wind, compete with the lightning, and fly as rapidly as thought itself. Labor seizes the thoughts of genius and the discoveries of science, and renders them pregnant with power. Labor sits in palaces of crystal. Labor makes civilization smile, liberty glad and humanity rejoice."

This is the description given of labor and its benefits. It is graphic, but true. Yet to eat the bread is considered a higher distinction than to grow the wheat of which it is made, to wear a silk dress than to weave the silk, to dwell in, and own a house than to build it. Indebted to the sons of honest manual labor are the records of science, and those useful inventions which serve the conveniences of life and promote civilization. If we turn to antiquity—Esop was a slave, Plautus a grinder of corn, Protagoras a porter, Virgil a farmer, so likewise was Sir Isaac Newton; Linneaus, the botanist, was a shoe maker, Franklin was a tallow chandler, and as we all know, especially indebted to labor is America, for three of the greatest rulers our country ever had. Abram Lincoln was a rail-splitter, Gen'l Grant was a tanner and James A. Garfield was once a carpenter boy.

"Honor and fame from no condition rise—
Act well your part and there all the honor lies."

I mention this because I know that not only is labor oppressed by capital, but it is frequently despised; so that among many it becomes a maxim, that to labor is degrading. Never mind how honest and intelligent the laborer, especially if he be what is called a manual laborer, he is excluded from the parlors of the wealthy, and has no lot or portion among our so-called "society people." The effect of this moral distemper is, that it affects even the "lower classes," so-called, and we hear this young woman refusing to keep company with one, because she is a washerwoman, and so it is with the young society man, he distinguishes in his society associations between the laboring man and the gentleman of leisure, and thus the virus spreads, until to *labor* is thought a degradation. Let us rather remember that "labor—all labor is noble and holy." What benefit would be gold or silver if labor did not produce the necessary comforts that money buys? Can a dollar by itself satisfy the cravings of hunger, shield the back from cold or give warmth to the frozen body? If the laborer is indebted to the capitalist for his money, the capitalist is indebted to the laborer for his produce.

Now I have attempted to describe capital and labor in their ordinary accepted terms and uses and as they are practically seen and experienced in their influences. The conclusion is inevitable, that we owe all that we are as individuals, representing wealth or as a nation in our commercial status, to labor. In short, that labor is essential to progress. And yet what do we find?—that for centuries these two important factors of human progress and advancement have been, and still are, in conflict. In the United States, as in foreign lands, the battle wages strong and fiercely. Labor has cried out from its humble quarters for justice and equality. It knows its power and its necessity, and it demands its rights. The poor laboring man sees no just reason why, by reason of the inadequate compensation he receives for his labor, he should forever remain poor, and die poor, and leave his family poor. He knows that by reason of his labor, of whatever kind, the dollar of the capitalist is made to produce two. He lives and sees the capitalist enjoy all the luxuries of life in superabundance; that he rides his fine horse and drives his coach and pair, richly caparisoned, that he lives in palaces, that his sons and daughters dress in silk and fine linen, in purple and gold, adorned with diamonds and other precious stones. He sees capital enjoying the benefits of knowledge, by the facility it has to buy books and pay for instruction and enjoy travel and observation. He sees the power it wields in the halls of legislation; and then labor turns and looks at *itself*, and what does it see? A squalid house, which frequently it does not own; the inability to keep but one pair of boots, and but one suit of decent clothes. After a day's labor and a return to home, with no chandelier to illumine the path; no Persian rug to put the worn and tired feet upon; no books or papers to improve his own mind nor his family's; no surplus fund to enable him to send his boy to college or to teach his daughters the refinements in the arts and graces of life, nor to afford him to attend the theatre, and thus relieve the tension of a day's muscular labor by entertaining and refreshing the mind in some elevating play of the famous Bard of Avon. No! none of this! None whatever; for, after paying his weekly rent to some Shylock of a landlord, who stands at the door, one hand opened for his "pound of flesh," and the other with the warrant of ejectment, if it is not delivered, and after settling with his grocer for the ordinary articles of food used during the week, then the shoemaker for repairing the shoes of three or four little ones, and the numerous other provisions for sustaining life too well known to need mentioning, he finds right surely he has not even a penny to give to the Lord in church next Sunday.

This is the relative position between capital and labor in this country, and it is the source of well nigh all of our social evils. It is capital oppressing labor that produces the serf in Russia, the communist in France, the anarchist of America. It is capital and its oppression of labor that disfranchises thousands of colored voters in the South. Does any one believe that the thousands of colored voters who have now no voice in the government of the states of which they are citizens, except as permitted by the representatives of capital, the Bourbons of the South, would long endure this political vassalage if they did not find themselves body and soul belonging, in one way or the other, to the powers of capital? In days gone by capital fitted out ships and paid wages to seamen in the holy commerce of buying and selling human flesh. It imposed the hardest and meanest labor, and when performed gave compensation in the lash or the chains. It then ground the Negro to death physically; it now grinds him, in common with his white brother, to death, morally, socially and politically. Against these evils labor has cried out loud and long, but capital has paid no heed. The profits of the Pacific Railroad continue to be forty millions, while the poor man's wages remain low and inadequate to his wants. And now comes the question, What is the *true* remedy? There are many remedies proposed, some of them tried, others have not; but there is one true remedy, and right here upon the threshold of this department of my discourse let me say that the true remedy is not to be found in mobs, neither in violence towards the oppressor, and least of all in the usurpation of the laws of the land. These are not remedies, but hindrances, and severe ones, too. The remedy is protection to labor and to American industries.

Mr. Henry George, who, among the advocates of the rights of labor, is the noblest Roman among them all, the purest and most unselfish of labor rights advocates, has in his profound work entitled "Progress and Poverty," most elaborately and learnedly discussed the errors which have long been entertained among political economists concerning the true rights and relationship between capital and labor, and to my mind has put to flight many a false theory. He has shown that wages are not drawn from capital, as many suppose, but from the produce of labor, and that the functions of capital are only to assist labor in production. So far, he is to my mind right. He then shows that the following remedies which have been proposed are inefficient, namely, "Greater economy in government. Combinations of workmen. Co-operation. Governmental direction and interference. A more general distribution of land," and then concludes with what the eminent author denominates "The *true remedy*," namely, "*We must make land common property.*" None other but the highest sentiments and conception of justice, and the equality of rights, could have produced so lofty a thought. I am not prepared to say it is error, but I am constrained to believe that it is impracticable. What we have to do is with the living present, and the practicability of the remedy offered. I am of opinion that the *true remedy* is the combination of workmen to the end of producing the co-operation of labor and capital to more equitable results. In other words, the true remedy is *labor organization*. It is true that Mr. Henry George declares against combination, because he says its remedy is not universal, but special, and at the expense of remedying a small part at the expense of the remainder of the whole; but to my mind there can be such a combination as will produce a universal remedy.

Such a combination is to be found in an organization or organizations, which truly have for their end and purpose, reform in the use of capital. It is *not* to be found in labor organizations of whatever kind which are based on selfish ends, and on discrimination on account of color and caste prejudice. To illustrate, if a labor organization in any place seeks to make a strike in order to raise the wages of its own workmen, without regard to what effect such action would have on other laborers, then such a course would be selfish and not in the light of reform. If again, an organization of brick masons should exclude, as some do, the colored citizen because of his color, despite he is as good and capable a workman as his white fellow workman, such an organization would not be in the light of reform, but would need reform itself, because if labor requires protection against the wrongs of capital, it needs it as a whole, and in whatsoever class of persons represented. Can labor afford to be divided against itself? If it is, it cannot stand, and utterly futile will be all the organizations of laborers throughout the country. Not only concert of action would be destroyed, but what is more essential, unity of action would be impracticable, for the laborer must feel that he is working for some common good ere he will co-operate with any organization.

It may be inquired, why are there at the present time such organizations as labor organizations? Have not capital and labor got along together for centuries without this opposition? True; but capital prospered and continued its oppression towards labor because of the ignorance of labor. Knowledge was not so universal as now, and the spirit of liberty of thought and action had not been so fully possessed by all classes. Then kings and emperors and despots ruled, instead of men chosen by the voice of the whole people. The spirit of republicanism, as is found embodied in the American Constitution, has given birth to a new era among men, which pervades nearly the whole civilized world. The art of printing, the press, and the school house have been the principal levers. When, one hundred years ago, but one in ten could read the views of Mr. Henry George or Mr. Powderly, or of any other reformer, now more than one-half can do so. It is not astonishing then to find men revolting against their poverty and seeking the cause of it, when they read and contemplate the following truths, as asserted by Mr. George, who says: "The man who works for another for stipulated wages in money, works under a contract of exchange. He also creates his wages as he renders his labor. During the time he is earning the wages he is advancing capital to his employer; but at no time, unless wages are paid before work is done, is the employer advancing capital to him." The lesson sought to be given is that money and labor are reciprocally necessary for the production of capital, and one has no claim greater than the other, and that, aside from thriftlessness or direct loss, one should not possess more than the other, neither in influence nor wealth. Now, how many persons who labored knew this fifty years ago.

Was not the popular belief that labor could do nothing without capital, and that capital had some distinct and higher mission in this life, more so than labor? That it is the privilege of capital to rule and labor to obey; capital to command and labor to serve. It is, then, to instruct the laboring classes in their rights that labor organizations should be formed — formed for reform for every branch of human activity, wherein, by reason of wealth, the poor are oppressed. They should be formed to reform the laws of the country when they are disadvantageous to the laboring classes, when they deprive one class of rights which another class exclusively enjoy. From this view, then, they must be of a semi-political character, for it is useless to secure rights by organization or combination, when you cannot protect them by law. The power of the labor party in this country and its influence are both unmeasured and unconceived.

It is capital that creates intemperance, because it gives opportunity for leisure and debauchery. I will now discuss my last topic, namely, "The true relationship of the Negro to all labor organizations." I am sorry to have to make this special reference, but the facts as they exist compel me to do so. It is well known that in America the white brother discriminates against his black brother on account of his color. This discrimination is to be found in nearly all vocations in life. Since the organization of labor societies this discrimination is to be found among some of them also, so that we are beginning to have what is known as colored labor organizations and white labor organizations, and the latter in some places refuse to admit to their organization the colored man. Now, there is no other ground for this distinction but caste prejudice, the blight of American civilization.

The Negro's relation to labor in this country is not that of a stranger, but a close friend. There is no department of labor in which he is not to be found, skilled or unskilled. The riches of this country as represented, not only in individuals, but also as a government, owe their development as well to Negro labor as to the labor of the white man. He is seen alongside of the

Irish, the German, the Swede and French, in the macadamization of our roads, as well as in the college. He is with and are of the carpenters and bricklayers, who build our houses; he is down in the mine with the white miners, and upon the surface of the earth, the rail road and the iron bridge; he erects the telegraph pole and stretches the wire from city to city, and state to state. He is in our manufactories as well as in our fields. He is a part of the capital producing force of *this* and other countries. He is then a laborer, with all the rights and privileges belonging thereto; but he is considered by many only fitted to work as a menial, and is denied equal opportunity with his white bretheren to defend and protect his labor. He is regarded as not entitled to equal wages with his white fellow workman, and is discriminated against in the payment of wages for like labor as performed by the white man. He is allowed to join the labor associations in some parts of the country, but not to associate upon an equal footing with his white brother. He is required to organize separate labor associations, and to be bound by all the rules and regulations of his white brothers' association in the sense of being regarded as subsidiary in his powers.

He must vote with his white brother, and be ready to fall in line when a strike is called; but when employment is offered, or the oppressing capitalist concludes to submit to terms, and should discriminate in his choice of selecting workmen, and reject the Negro, there is no rule requiring his white brother to resist the discrimination as a discrimination against labor on account of color. He is not regarded as entitled to office or participation in the labor organizations among white men. He is denied accommodations in public places where his white brother laborer supinely enters without remonstrance, and thus in these instances, and many more which I could mention, the Negro's relationship to labor organizations in this country is a false one, and while in such a condition not advantageous to him. He is desired to be used as a tool for the work of reform, to benefit a class of laborers who divide themselves from the Negro laborer on the simple ground of color. Is a union with such organizations profitable to him? *Is* there a union where there is such a distinction, in which there is always a difference in favor of one party and against the other? I say no. It is then better that the colored citizen keep aloof from such organizations unless he can be received and treated as the equal of any other man or member.

It is to the very great advantage of all labor organizations that they include the representatives of labor without distinction or discrimination. The wrongs of the laboring man affect them *all;* the rights, when secured, should benefit *all*. To secure the needful remedy a great battle must be waged against capital; and the ammunition needed is not, as I have already said, mobs nor violence, guns nor powder; but firmness, manhood, perseverance, self sacrifice, union, good faith to all, and *numbers*. Nothing else than these *all* combined can afford to attempt a battle against money. If numbers are necessary, numbers as would be increased by the addition of the colored citizen to all labor organizations, must be respected. It is not only the co-operation of the colored man with the white in the reform of labor, in securing adequate wages, which is needed; but it is needed by the addition of his vote also. It will tell where reform is needed in legislation, where men who in office respect not labor in the execution of the laws, or the administration of the same.

But there is also a moral good in the union of the two races in the work of labor reform. In union there is strength. In co-association there is development. The elevation of the colored citizen to the plane of the white man's industry is something which no good and patriotic citizen should deny him. He is a part of the American people. He is in America to stay, and it is utter folly to try to keep him down. Those who are endeavoring to do so are certain of defeat. I am not writing as the eulogist of the colored citizen; but who can deny his progress in the short time of a quarter of a century? From a chattel under the law to a man, a freeman, and a citizen under the constitution; from a poor man without food and shelter in 1865 to a tax paying citizen of $30,000,- 000 of property in Louisiana and $10,000,000 in Georgia—States in which proud aristocratic capital walked and stalked and put its iron heel on the Negro in every shape and form. Has he not a right, with every other son of labor, to assert his rights and to seek to protect them? This none will deny and prove the denial. Again, the signs of the times show that the two races, in matters of material progress, are fast coming together. They are homogeneous in their aims of development. In nearly every business occupation in which the white brother is found the black brother is entering upon. He is in commerce, he is in art, he is in science, and he is in industry. If his whole body is not in he has got in his head, and no pulling can get him out. Let there be union between the laborers in both races, and let exact and equal justice be done all. Let them work together for a common good. Labor organizations are not citadels of crime, as some think, but they are legitimate operations.

Amasa Walker, whom I have so often quoted, because he is the most advanced American thinker on the relation of capital to labor, says: "Under a government acknowledging the rights of all men, the laborer must, of course, have the same rights as his fellow citizens, neither more nor less. He asks no favor, and grants none. He demands the same justice, the same freedom accorded to others. He should be able, so far as law is concerned, to work when and for whom he chooses. * * * The laborer is not under obligation to act as an insulated individual any more than the capitalist. If the latter is permitted to combine with his fellows in order to enhance the power and profits of capital, it is equally the right of the laborer to do the same, and equally the duty of the legislator to give him any facilities for doing this he may justly demand. If capital is incorporated, labor should have the same privilege. If favors in any case are awarded to one party, they should certainly be furnished to the other. Laborers, then, may combine, if they deem it best, to act in concert in regard to their interests." It is plain that if the colored man is to be kept out of labor organizations, or discriminated against, labor itself must be divided, conflict will ensue, as it has already done in many cases. Can a colored laborer, who has been denied admission into a labor organization, or feels that his rights have been discriminated against on account of his color, be blamed for throwing himself across the path of labor reform and obstructing it, by accepting employment for wages which the members of some labor organization have refused? If he join the ranks of the enemy, it is because they are to him a friend when he is driven away from the doors of labor reform. He simply, in accepting lower wages, uses the *lex talionis*, agreed in war to be the legitimate weapon of self-defense. The true relationship, then, of the Negro to all labor organization is *that of an equal*, enjoying the same rights and privileges as his white brother, and entitled to the same protection and benefits. Anything less than this makes labor in its work of reform proscriptive and disadvantageous to the Negro in the shape of labor organizations. It is better that he hew out his race-destiny alone, than aid in his own degradation.

The true relationship of the Negro to all labor

organizations, should be one of perfect harmony between the two races, a development the consummation of which is devoutly to be wished for, and the benefits to be derived incalculable, in the light of our composite nationality. In the language of faithful Ruth of old, when asked to leave those among whom she had lived and gleaned, we say to you, our white brethren, working for the amelioration of labor, "Entreat me not to leave thee, or return from following thee, for whithersoever thou goest I will lodge; thy people shall be my people, and thy God my God; where thou diest I will die, and there will I be buried." Yes, America is the home of the African equally as it is the home of the German, the Irishman, the Frenchman and the Russian. It is the home of the Jew and the Gentile alike, the Greek and the Roman. It is the land of the free and the home of the brave. Upon its shores not a single fetter binds the limb of the slave. In the language of Hon. R. B. Elliott who, in his speech on the Civil Rights bill in Congress in 1872, truly said: "The time is not far distant when all of our fellow citizens, whether they be native born, or whether they first drew the breath of life on the banks of the Shannon or of the Rhine; whether they sprang from the Orient or the Occident, no longer swayed by unjust prejudices, * shall be touched with the inspiration of a holier sentiment, and shall recognize the universal fatherhood of God and the universal brotherhood of man." The South needs know these truths.

But is not this seen now in the shape, like as a

cloud, not bigger than a man's hand, upon the horizon? Who can fail to discover this universal brotherhood as it grows and spreads among us, when we read how Grand Master Workman Powderly, of the Knights of Labor, recognized his "brother in black" in Richmond, during the late convention held there. By his actions and by his words he became the Man of the Period in America—the beacon light of future progress, justice and equality, in the United States, among all her citizens. Hear him give his reasons for recognizing Mr. Farrell, a colored man. He says: "My sole object in selecting a colored man to introduce me, was to encourage and help to uplift his race from a bondage worse than that which held him in chains twenty-five years ago, namely, mental slavery. I desired to impress upon the minds of white and black, that the same result followed the action in the field of labor, whether that action was on the part of Caucasian or Negro labor. * * You stand face to face with a stern living reality, a responsibility which cannot be avoided or shirked. * * The Negro is free. He is here and he is here to stay. He is a citizen and must learn to manage his own affairs. His labor and that of the white man must be thrown upon the market side by side, and no human eye can detect the difference. * * Both claim an equal share in the protection afforded to American labor, and both mechanics must sink their differences, or else fall a prey to the slave labor now being imported to this country." Do you hear this, my Southern white friend who, while laboring, can yet scarcely earn, through low wages, enough to educate your child or support your family, yet cry out against the association of the Negro in the means of uplifting and protecting labor, and support free trade?

Mr. Powderly continues: "I have a strong desire to see the black man educated. Southern labor, regardless of its color, must learn to read and write. * * * The equality of American citizenship is all that we insist upon, and that equality must not be trampled upon. * * * To the Convention I say, let no member surrender an iota of intellectual freedom because of any clamor. Hold fast to that which is true and right. The triumph of noise over reason is but transient. Our principles will be better known, if not today, it may be tomorrow. In the field of labor and American citizenship we recognize no line of race, creed, politics or color."

What words of burning truth? How fearless the man. All honor and praise to his good name, whose undying fame shall last as long as the eternal truth. He is a wonderful counsellor among men as to their earthly welfare. His wisdom is above many. He is the friend of the poor and the oppressed. Long may he live! Let me advise that the colored laborer and the white laborer unite as equals in this work of reform, for

> United we stand, divided we fall;
> Union of heart, freedom to all.
> Throughout the world our motto shall be,
> *Vive l'Amerique*—home of the free.

These views the "New South" needs, and more.

Equitable adjustment between capital and labor is the true source of its future development.

Before closing this chapter let me advert to what seems to me both pertinent and important in the relation of capital and labor, as they must affect the "New South." I mean by this the topic of a tariff on commerce or trade. Without attempting to enter upon the vast details in proof, or claiming any ability to even measurably discuss so vast and intricate, as well as so vexed a topic in public affairs and in political economy so differently viewed, I yet venture to call attention to the "New South's," as I view it, highest interest, and that is to promote its welfare in the spread and advancement of its industries by the safest means possible.

The "New South," when investigated, reveals truly and above all other things its industrious growth. Every year new industries spring up within its midst. Manufactories are to be found in every principal city and town in the South today. The mineral resources of the South are vast, its water power is extensive, and already capitalists from the North, East and West show their willingness to introduce their capital and develop the South. Birmingham and Anniston, Ala.; Charleston, Columbia, Graniteville, Greenville, Orangeburg and Aiken, S. C.; Durham, Greensboro and Wilmington, N. C., are among the numerous evidences of the influence of Northern capital upon Southern soil. But among these industries are such productions as not only find a home market, but are brought into competition with foreign productions of a like kind. And just here capital and labor in America ought to come together for self-protection. In the South this protection should be with an eye to future interests. Brush away all the cobwebs of intricacy concerning the question of a protective tariff and free trade, as discussed by political economists, and bring the question down to a common sense basis, and ask the question: Will the unrestricted introduction of foreign industries like those of our own in America, brought into competition with ours, lessen wages and decrease capital at home, or not? Are either the American manufacturer or laborer benefited by free trade?

To the South the question is, under a new social *regime* wherein free labor has supplanted involuntarily servitude, and thus makes every pound of cotton cost more to grow and harvest by free labor, than it did by slave labor, and in view of the fact of the new development of your industries in the manufacture of well nigh every article that the North has manufactured and become rich thereby under—a protective tariff. I say, under these circumstances, is it wise that the South advocate a policy which will stagnate its industries and pauperize its laboring population? No question is so common in its interests as this, and it ought to be, and will be, the future political issue of the South, in which we shall find buried race, prejudice or color distinction; for it is the laboring man's question and interest without regard to color, as it is the capitalist's without regard to locality. Low wages means starvation, taxation without the means of paying taxes, inability to support church or State. Indeed, free trade will not even admit of "taxation for revenue only." Why should England rejoice if free trade in America, with whom possibly the largest commercial intercourse is carried on, is not beneficial to her? Is she so contented with our treaty upon the fisheries, or is she not constantly violating them because they restrict her commerce.

But these views are simply limited as in this volume to show how the "New South," investigated, discovers far more important issues than are those kept alive today by the South as necessary to its advancement. With the large Negro population of the South, dividing itself as other races have hiterto done, as free men, into the land holder, the capitalist and the laborer, skilled or otherwise, this class of citizens must, too, have a deep interest in the protection of labor, not only in relation to capital, but also as it meets with foreign competition in its productions and in its exercise at home. Let the Negro and the poor white man look to the protection of labor in the South, while the capitalist seeks to protect his dollar invested from foreign minimization.

CHAPTER IX.

THE NEGRO—PAST, PRESENT AND FUTURE.

No treatment of the South can be considered efficient which does not mark the progress of the Negro citizen. In the following remarks I have discussed the Negro without regard to his present location, because it must be admitted that wherever in America the Negro is to be found, he can be traced with very few exceptions, if any, to the South. It was the cradle of his earlier existence. The starting point of his future progress. Hence I deem it not inappropriate to discuss this element in connection with my views on the "New South," so that if not directly, yet indirectly, we may connect this class of citizenship with the progress of the South.

As a distinct race of people, our past and present are known to us—our future is conjecture, based on human experience and observation.

The introduction of slavery into America marks the time from which the impartial judge may gather his earliest views of the colored man in this country, his condition then, his present advancement, and his probable future. For more than two hundred years the condition of slavery existed in America. Slavery means the subjugation of all human rights by force or intrigue, and without being the punishment for crime. Such a system has naturally the effect of obstructing all development in intellect, mind, morals and industry. Some people have strangely called slavery a schoolmaster unto freedom. How it can appear that slavery, with its cruelties and its hindrances to human development, save in muscle, to that stage and condition for which God created man, was a schoolmaster, is beyond my comprehension. This idea belongs to the period and the men who think that the more whipping you give a child, the better man or woman you make of him or her; or, as the old Dutchman who thought that his child had said "damn," but finding he had not, said, "Neffer mind, sir; I am going to whip you for tinking damn." Let us look a little while into this so-called school house, and see what work was done. For nearly two hundred years the slave was engaged as a manual laborer only, tilling the soil being his chief employment. Thousands and tens of thousands of acres of Southland have been cultivated by the Negro, the staple produce being cotton. The revenue derived from this labor enriched the South, supported its churches, its colleges and universities, built its houses and gave all comfort and luxury to the master, who in his kingly palace, in purple and gold, looked down upon the lowly slave in his cabin, and in darkness of ignorance, without the light of education.

His condition was little better than that of the beast of burden. He was worked and then sold at the pleasure of his master, and worked again and sold by his new master. Domestic society, the primitive form of social government, in which the graces and virtues are commenced and developed, was in its crudest form as seen by him. Today at home, tomorrow a stranger in a strange land. The family tie was constantly snapped asunder until it became weak. Husband separated from wife without their consent, children from parents, brother from sister. The acquisition of knowledge in letters was denied. The school house was a sealed book to the slave. The acquisition of property was denied him. Not owning himself he could own nothing else. For two hundred years of labor the slave acquired not a foot of land nor a single dollar which he could call his own, except in isolated cases where he was allowed to labor and buy himself. The arts of industry were kept from him, except as he was taught the mechanical arts for the benefit of his master. It would not do to teach the slave the arts of industry, because industry leads to independence, no more than it was wise to teach him letters, because knowledge is power. The religion taught the slave was that of obedience to his master only. Shut out from the civilizing influences of cultivated society and contact with intelligence, he remained a dwarf in manhood, and is not in this respect full grown even today. The scraping of the foot, the hat under the arm, and the manner of resenting an insult—which is by running off at a safe distance, sometimes in the wood, and then swear and curse the trees and shoot at the stars—and the content to live and be shot down and lynched without strong combined resistance, are evidences in the South today that the Negro's manhood in that portion of the country is not yet fully developed. Slavery taught fear; fear begat misconfidence, which is the greatest blight resting upon the Negro today. This is traceable direct to the influence of slavery. It has incorporated itself into the man and woman of the race, and books and figures will never eradicate it. It is physcological and must wait the eflux of time and environment. What we need to change this condition is contact with higher and purer life.

Says Herbert Spencer: "Whatever amount of power an organism expends in any shape, is the correlate and equivalent of a power that was taken into it from without." Thus it is about slavery and its consequences. For two hundred years it inculcated weakness, misconfidence, and envy and jealousy in the slave. It is now expending its correlate distrust, disunion and dependence in freedom. How long could slavery have existed if all the slaves had been united to destroy it? Did not every attempt at its overthrow fail—from Nat Turner to John Brown—for the want of unity in the Negro himself? Thus it is seen that slavery was a poor schoolmaster unto freedom. But let us now contrast slavery with freedom, or the past with the present. After a period of more than two hundred years of bondage, a race of people who had been brought from their native country into this country and held as slaves, was made free. Their emancipation was the result of a combination of causes and circumstances well known to the reader of American history, and to those who have lived during or at the time. Concerning this period, so eventful in the life of the young Republic, so fraught with vital interests concerning the perpetuity of the nation, I have only to say, it marked the period of a transition from national death to a resurrection and a new life. This period is known as the end of the civil war, and the commencement of reconstruction of the "New South." Politically, this refers to the legislative adjustment of the several States which had been in rebellion against the Union. I say legislative, because the laws of reconstruction never were received by the South except as through force. It is but lately that there are some signs of an honest acceptance of the situation which makes us one people. Time will bring this all right, I trust.

But reconstruction did more than reconstruct the states politically—it reconstructed, or sought to reconstruct, the two races. The white man was brought back to his proper relationship as a citizen with the Federal Union, while the Negro was returned to the status of a free man—the condition in which he was made by God. By Act of Congress he was made a citizen. The ballot was in his hand—his destiny was his own making. Circumscribed though they were, his opportunities for moral, religious and industrial development, were enlarged by his freedom. His social relationship was changed from that of slave to master, from that of bondman to freeman; from chattel to a recognized human being under the law. He moved along with his white fellow citizen as an equal under the law, yet he was poor and ignorant. But the former master looked upon his former slave with envy and chagrin—and this was natural. It was property loss—value destroyed. Again, the relationship of master and slave being so dissimilar, an immediate acceptance of the new relationship could not be expected, hence we should look at much that was done in wrong and violence towards the Negro by his former master after freedom, not so much on account of color as condition and relationship. It was this belief acted upon, which shut him out from all participation in civilization with his white fellow citizen.

He therefore entered upon the stage of freedom, the race of progress and the march of civilization, burdened with two hundred years of the effect of slavery. No mental nor moral training, no light. His earliest need was light to see and opportunity to move. He needed intellectual light, moral light, religious light, political light, and industrial light. His intellectual light was first sought after, along with his religious training, by those who not only believed in his capacity to learn, but in this necessity preparatory to his entering upon the responsibility of citizenship. I have always felt that this was a strong plea, weak only in its discrimination. It was but right in any government, State or National, to make a just prerequisite for its citizens entering upon so sacred a responsibility as to govern by his ballot, but I cannot see the difference between an ignorant black voter and an ignorant white one.

But the education of the colored man, I would say, has been fundamentally defective from the beginning. It is to be observed that, despite the knowledge of letters by a large class of our youth, especially in the South, they yet show a subserviency and a want of aspiration and just pride, arising from the fact that they have been educated in the knowledge of the power and elevation of another race only, and nothing about their own. There is enough history of the Negro race to make a Negro proud of his race. It is to be found in the history of Egypt, Assyria, Babylon, Greece and Rome, aye, even and throughout Africa itself. Why not then teach the Negro child more of himself and less of others, more of his elevation and less of his degradation. *This* only can produce true pride of race, which begets mutual confidence and unity.

To do this our school books must be changed, so that the two races may know more fully of one onother. The history of Washington should be followed by that of Toussaint l'Overture; the poems of Bryant and Longfellow, by those of Phillis Wheatley, George W. Williams' History of the United States, as well as Bancroft's History of the United States.

I do not mean by this that the knowledge of Anglo-Saxon literature, art and science should be disregarded. It is the Thesaurus out of which only can we find the necessary treasures of knowledge, but it does not contain all the knowledge, power and literature of the human family. The past gave but little opportunity to the colored man to advance, not only intellectually, but morally, socially or industrially. Where slavery existed, there could be no true standard of morals. Slavery was the enemy of good morals, because it taught a false relationship between man and his brother and man and God. The evil influence of slavery upon the morals of the slave is yet to be found in a large portion of the colored race, especially in the South. The marriage tie, which was impracticable in slavery, is still disregarded in many respects, and that unit of society, the home, still is in a low condition in many parts.

Some of us do not seem to remember or to know that our home is the index of our social lives, and that we should make it as beautiful and as comfortable as we can. From a clean house will generally come a well dressed man, woman or child, and the converse is equally true. Much of the duty concerning home should be taught in our schools and churches. A dirty clad child should not be admitted into school.

Our next and last burden of the past is our social condition. I do not mean by this what is commonly called "social equality," but our condition as a part of the body politic. The gulf which existed in slavery between the white and colored brother has truly not widened; but the chasm yet exists. A white man in the South feels he is degraded by any social contact whatever with his black brother. He will not consent to work with him even in the very lowest occupation, as an equal and side by side, and the question presents itself, why is this? Why will a white man sit by the side of a Negro coachman, as coachman, and not by the side of him as a traveler on a railroad car, or in a hotel, or on a steamboat? Is it because of his color? Not at all. It is because the colored man is still viewed through the eye of the past, and his condition is regarded as an inferior one, because he was once a slave. This is not irremediable, as I will hereafter show, but it will take some time before the pyschological condition of the white man can be changed in this respect, and this change must commence in the church. Separate churches teach separate schools, and distinctions on railroads and the like. The church must answer for all this at the last day, and the plea "Am I my brother's keeper?" will not do. It is the duty of the church to preach the common brotherhood of man and common Fatherhood of God, but it does not. Instead of this, it is engaged in teaching the curse and inferiority of a race which the blood of Christ seems unable to wipe out in the estimation of some professing christianity.

The bald injustice towards the colored voter in the South today, is that he is not allowed to exercise his suffrage in the South without restraint, because it is said he is ignorant; while his ignorant white fellow citizen goes unrestricted, or at least unmolested, in his igno-

for the social distinctions which exist. It is because of our inequality of condition. Equality rance. In the work of educating the enfranchised slave and fitting him for citizenship, strong minded men and women entered after reconstruction amid persecutions and oppressions untold. This work was supplemented by the Freedmen's Bureau as an agent of the Federal Government. Why did the white man of the South oppose the education of the ex-slave as he did, after his emancipation? The answer is plain. It is because knowledge is power, and in his ignorance the Negro could easily be controlled. The greatest mistake concerning the early education of the Negro in the South was the indifference paid to the education of the adult class. The laboring class being ignorant and not being able to read and write, became an easy prey to the intriguer and deceiver, and this is so even today. No better and more useful amendment to the system of education in the South could be established in the present time than the opening of night schools to teach the adult Negro population how to read and write. This would prevent much litigation and expense and promote the financial interest of our laboring fellow man, both black and white. If every colored man in the South could read and write, sign his own lien, deed or mortgage, write his receipt and make his contract himself, his progress in money, lands and houses in the next twenty years, would be double what it is today.

But there is another and very important reason

restores the equilibrium, and none can fail to see how by education in letters, morals and culture, the Negro is compelling a just recognition of this equality. And now that we have briefly reviewed the history of the past, and seen its hindrances toward our elevation, let us look into the present, and see what advancement we have made. First, in the past we were illiterate and without education. How are we today? Not a quarter of a century has passed since our freedom, and yet during the past twenty-four years the Negro has reached a stage in the knowledge of letters which is the marvel of all men. He is now to be found in the school house as pupil, as well as in the college and university. By hook or by crook, and in spite of all obstacles, he has drunk from the springs of learning in the highest institutions in the land, and is now fitted to be the instructor of his race in their own schools and colleges. In science, in art, in invention, in music, in history, in painting, in the drama, in the field of journalism, and in government, has he entered the field, and his progress is to be seen by any impartial judge. Let us look at his progress a little, statistically. It is said that since 1863 until the present time, the progress of the colored man is seen in the following: There are now in the Southern States alone sixteen thousand colored teachers, one million pupils, sixty Normal schools, fifty colleges and universities, and twenty-five theological seminaries. In the North, East and West the education of the colored man has been far in advance of that in the South. He has graduated from Yale, Dartmouth, Ann Arbor, and other prominent institutions of learning, and by association and capacity, has won a position high among his fellow white brethren in education.

The Rev. Dr. Hartzell, D. D., speaking at Ocean Grove, in 1883, before the Convention of Christian Educators met there, said: "The progress of the Negro in America since Emancipation has been marvellous. They came out of slavery poor in body, mind and soul. Their bodies were cursed with generations of degredation — not labor, for that, if followed as it should be, is ennobling; but of unnatural labor, where every refinement of taste and habit was sacrificed to the demand for muscular endurance. Their minds were cursed with generations of enforced ignorance. * * * To understand anything of the progress of this race since Emancipation we must look into the depths of the mind in which freedom found them. * * * With only a few individual or family exceptions the great body of the Negroes came out of slavery absolutely penniless, and with scarcely enough rags to cover their nakedness, with every influence of Church and State and commerce and social life opposed to their freedom, and a determination by their former masters that, if not slaves, their future of right ought to be, and *must* be, one of dependent subserviency to the white race." How true this description? Indeed, the problem to be solved today is, Shall the Negro be forever "hewers of wood and drawers of water" for another race, or be an independent race of people, working out their own destiny? This question must be solved sooner or later, or the annihilation of the Negro or internecine strife will follow. No race of people, as soon as they become intelligent enough to know their rights, will stand a deprivation of them. "But," continues Dr. Hartzell, "whatever progress the freedmen have made has been chiefly because of the splendid qualities they possess in spite of great disadvantages. Whatever helps have come to them, they have laid hold of with tremendous faith and tenacity. They are climbing up into the higher realms of learning. Their mathematicians are mastering Hamilton and communing with Newton."

This splendid testimony is but just and true, and is remarkable as coming from the race which, as a whole, has opposed the Negro's advancement in education. We are asked for proof of the Negro's advancement. We answer, go into Yale, Ann Arbor, Harvard, Princeton, Oberlin and Howard University. Consult their record in the past twenty years and see if the Negro has not shown not only his capacity, but his advancement. See the schools of the Negro's own establishment, namely, Wilberforce, Paul Quinn, Morris Brown, Selma University, the State University of Louisville, Ky., Livingstone College, N.C., and Allen University, of Columbia, S.C., and see what he has done there. In this short period he has acquired the knowledge of law, medicine, theology and art. In the drama, music, sculpture and painting, he now vies with his white brother. He has entered the councils of the nation and assisted in making its laws. He has ascended the judicial bench and become part of the expounders of law. He has even entered the domain of the Executive and executed the law. In the courts of foreign nations he has appeared as the representative of his country—his native land—protected its international rights, and then returned home, only to find himself deprived of his own rights. The names of Douglas Langston, Bruce, Elliott, Cain, Price and Lynch; Ruffin, Morriss Chester, Pinchback, Tanner, Cromwell, Grimke, Fortune, Stewart, Perry, Brawley, Simmons, Scarborough, and a host of others, form a galaxy of men; and Frances E. Harper, Copin Morsell, Vinton Davis, Preston Ray, Madam Selika, Nellie Brown, and others, are women who shall shine as lights upon the pages which must occupy the future history of the Negro race in America. In the Church, men eminent in virtue and ability, have arisen in this short period. I need only mention the names of Revs. Campbell, Brown, Ward, Turner, Dickerson, Steward, Embry, Lee, and others of the A. M. E. Church; Holly, Cromwell, Grimke, Simmons, and many others, to show what we have done in this respect. And yet some critics say the Negro is incapable of intellectual advancement—he will die out; while others fear we will increase in numbers so rapidly as to blacken the whole American continent. These chimera are the talks of fanatics.

So far as our numerical increase is concerned, we will decrease in fecundity as we increase intellectually. Science proves this as well as history records the facts among other people. But we will also increase in power and intelligence, and this is more important to us than numbers. It is said we cannot advance, socially, morally, nor intellectually, without the association of a superior class. The Negro in America has negatived that assertion. He has advanced in spite of the forced disassociation of the so-called superior class. He has shown himself no parasite. I admit that co-association facilitates advancement and gives strength by unity, but this is upon the plane of equality. This has not been granted us yet.

But our progress may be viewed not only from an intellectual, but also from an industrial standpoint. As I have aforesaid, we came out of slavery poor and homeless, encountering all the difficulties which a disappointed and conquered people could throw in our way. Our ignorance made us victims to the crafty and dishonest, so that even the progress we have made in the accumulation of property might, nay, would, have been greater but for a systematized plan in the South to keep the Negro as poor as possible by cheating and defrauding him out of his earnings and preventing him, when possible, from becoming the owner of the soil.

I once heard a prominent Senator in the South say, speaking to a large audience chiefly of white people, "Keep the spelling book and the land from the possession of the Negro, if you ever hope to control him." But in spite of all this we have made some progress as the result of our restricted opportunity in the work of industry.

John W. Cromwell, Esq., a colored lawyer of Washington, D. C., and journalist, has of late epitomised the history of the wealth of the Negro since freedom. He says: "In North Carolina there are twenty-two Negroes worth from $10,000 to $20,000 each. In South Carolina the Negroes own $10,000,000 worth of property. In Charleston, fourteen men represent $18,000. The family of the Noisette's, truck farmers, being worth $150,000. In the City Savings Bank in Charleston Negroes own in deposits $12,496. In Philadelphia, Mr. John McKee is said to be worth over a half million. In New York, Negroes are said to be worth from five to six million dollars worth of real property. In Louisiana Negroes pay tax on $15,000,000 in the City of New Orleans alone, and on $30,000,000 in the entire State. Mississippi has twenty-seven colored citizens worth a million of dollars. And thus we might continue, if space permitted, to show the vast progress of the Negro in spite of all disadvantages. Much of this savings has arisen from economy, thriftless as we are said to be. The washer-woman, the cook, the wood-cutter, the whitewasher, the farmer, the small merchant and the humble mechanic, represent these worths, and not the heirs of any wealthy ancestor. In skilled labor we are at the lowest stage of progress, because of the severe prejudice among white mechanics to labor with colored ones or to admit them as apprentices in the workshop. Since freedom the workshop and all other avenues of skilled industry have been closed against the Negro on account of color. He is allowed to carry the hod, but not to place the brick; to pull the bellows, but not to fashion the iron; to fire the engine, but not to guide the locomotive; to sweep the counting house, but not to keep the books; to ink the type, but not to set up the form. This is all done by a combination of men known as Trades Unionists, but who are in fact disunionists and destroyers of their country's welfare.

But in spite of all this, the Negro, like the boy who has been refused admittance to a circus or horse race, because he has no ticket, has got under the canvas, and is inside with his white opponent, seeing and learning. Argus-eyed while working with his hands, he has watched with his eyes and heard with his ears. When a few years ago our white brethren determined to show the development of American industry alongside with the industry of the world, the Negro was there. In nearly every department of industry he was represented in the New Orleans Expositions of 1884-5. From the making of a nail to that of a locomotive, from the toy whistle to the artistic organ. He not only ground the corn, but he made the flour. In this exhibition, I must also mention the wonderful progress of woman, whom man has said was made for domestic purposes only, I mean the colored woman, whom slavery and prejudice of color had shut out of all opportunity to learn even that which the colored man was permitted to know. The colored woman at the New Orleans Expositions showed her skill in needle-work, landscape painting, music, and many other refined arts. The great question now is, how shall we engage in the industrial arts of our country as free men and women? Some say this is a social question, and cannot be regulated by law, and that every man is master of his own skill. True; but no man who is a citizen should be allowed to retard the progress and welfare of his country. Wills are regulated by law. Acts involving the non-alienation of land would be regarded as void in this country. And why? Because they are against the spirit of republican institutions. So likewise is the practice of excluding anyone from entering the workshop because of his or her color.

But should this just privilege be not granted us, we must continue to make our way by our own energy. We have done much by ourselves, we can do more. The time has come when it is of the utmost importance that the Negro shall enter upon the industries of the age. It is first necessary to develop manhood and womanhood. A young man who has been to school, and has passed through a college or university curriculum, but who knows no trade or industrial pursuit, is but half developed. So likewise with a young woman. It won't do to be able to read Latin or Greek, if a man, or play the piano or paint a landscape, if a woman, and know nothing of building a house, or sewing on a button, or making a garment. Such are not fit for life, nor the duties of life; nay, such are not fit for citizenship. The idea that manual labor is degrading, is erroneous. Is it an insult to a college graduate if his mother asks him to cut a piece of wood, or his father should put him behind the plow; or if the young lady be required to wash a garment, cook a piece of meat, or sew on a button? But concerning industry, we must enlarge our knowledge herein, and the best means is the industrial annex. Let every pupil in every school learn some trade or art, and by this means our youth shall be ready for the time coming when merit, and not color, shall be the passport to fame, wealth and honor.

But before concluding evidence of our industrial advancement, let me call attention to the evidence of our industrial progress from an ecclesiastical standpoint. At the commencement of our freedom we were not only poor in houses, but in churches in which to worship God, and in school houses wherein we might get educated. The African Methodist Episcopal church, in 1816 was composed, by Dr. Jennifer's testimony, of only 17 members. In 1884 it had increased to 10 bishops, 7 general officers, 50 annual conferences, 150 presiding elders, 2,450 appointments, 2,732 churches, 390,000 members. The members of this denomination, in the short space of twenty years of freedom, expended for missions $25,000, for education $75,000, for education and religion $130,445. They own as church property upwards of a million of dollars, and receive and disburse quadriennially thousands. All this in fifty years of existence, and but twenty of these in freedom. Other religious denominations have made like progress.

In the past we had no political status, save as our numbers gave representation to our white masters in the council of the nation. Slavery grew defiant and became intolerant, spreading its blight in its path. It was a moral affliction, and it is truly said by another that "war may stride over the land with the crushing step of a giant; pestilence may steal over it like an invisible curse, reaching its victims silently and unseen, unpeopling here a village and there a city, until every dwelling is a sepulchre; famine may brood over it with a long and weary visitation, until the sky itself is brazen and the beautiful greenness gives place to a parched desert, a wide waste of unproductive desolation; but these are only physical evils. The wild flower will bloom in peace on the field of battle. * * * The destroying angel will retire when his errand is done, and the nation will again breathe freely, the barrenness of famine will cease at last, the cloud will be prodigal of its rain once hoarded, and the wilderness will blossom; but for moral desolation there is no reviving spring." Such was the effect of slavery upon our land, until God, through his servants, the Abolitionists, called a halt. He made Abram Lincoln his chosen messenger. The Missouri Compromise was disregarded, and the civil war ensued. It resulted in the emancipation of the Negro. He became a citizen, entitled under the law to the rights and privileges of citizenship, among these the ballot and the right to occupy and hold public office. Some have criticised the sudden thrusting of the grave responsibility of citizenship and suffrage upon the colored man uneducated. Let us look at the result. Has he brought his country to the condition of Rome, with all its learning? Did the scenes which led to the fall and decline of the Roman Empire ever stand at the door of government under Negro rule in the South? No, never! In the short space of twenty years of freedom the newly emancipated slave has entered Congress and the halls of legislation of the several States; he has sat upon the judicial bench and expounded the law; he has appeared at the bar as lawyer side by side with his former master; he has represented his country in foreign lands; he has been one of the guardians of the National Treasury, giving authority and validity to its currency by his signature in office; and in well nigh every department of the State and Nation he has entered upon some official duty as a new citizen. And I may challenge contradiction when I say no race of people upon the civilized globe has ever entered upon such responsible duties and proven themselves better fitted.

But I am reminded that the Negro in politics in the South gave it a corrupt government. I deny the charge. That there was corruption it is true, enough to lead to the fall which followed the G. O. P.; but the Negro was not the cause. His political enemies will admit that he was not. The true cause was political demagoguery of the so-called Negro leaders in the South, who loved money and office better than the preservation of the Republican party, the welfare of the country, or the true advancement of the Negro. The Republican party must not shake its gory locks at the Negro of the South and say, "Thou didst it." No, something "Haz-y" did it, and it has remained dark ever since.

And now I must complete my views upon our *social* condition. I mean by this our relationship with our fellow white brother in the walks of life. It is widely known that, because of his color, the Negro is deprived of entering into the society of his white brethren. I do not mean by this his dining room, his parlor, his ball room, or his reception. This is domestic regulation, of which every family or head is the sovereign; but I mean this, that we are deprived of accommodations in many public places, equal privileges on the railroads and on steamboats; that we are denied admission to the workshop, and refused the opportunity to learn trades; we are shut out from skilled labor of every description; we are denied employment in the counting house, or house of merchandise; the telegraph office, and all other places, except as menials. This is our present social condition in spite of what progress I have shown that we have made. And the question now is, How shall this injustice be remedied?

How shall the colored man and woman secure equal opportunity to become a useful citizen? To become sellers as well as buyers, landlords as well as tenants, authors as well as readers, producers as well as consumers, and to enter upon the industrial pursuits of life with equal privileges of any other citizen upon the American continent? He is told by some that he must "work out his own destiny." He has done a great deal toward this, as none will deny. He has more to do, it is true, but what he needs is *unfettered opportunity*, like his white brother citizen. The war cry for us is Opportunity! Opportunity! How shall this be secured? Our white fellow citizen can tell. He is in advance of us; will he let us come along with him? If not, why does he object? I have already shown that the objection to the Negro's progress is two-fold—pyschological and political. A train of years, in which the white man has been educated in the belief that we are an inferior race, is one cause. His love of power and control is the other. As to the former belief, it yet exists. Christian ministers are today found quoting scripture to prove that, as descendants of Ham, we are a cursed race, and declared to be the slave of slaves. How can their hearers believe else? But to my mind this problem can best be solved by ourselves. If believed an inferior race, let us prove ourselves an equal in energy, capacity and economy of life. When we cannot climb the mountain, let us tunnel the rock. Let us apply ourselves to every species of industry within our grasp. Our thoughts are ours, our muscle is now our own; what we need most is wisdom—how to combine and be strong as a people. We cannot do this if we are not UNITED as a race. Let us learn the ladder of success. It is made up of the following rounds: First, mutual confidence in each other. Second, unity. Third, industry, which means application of thought to labor. Fourth, education, or the knowledge how to apply. Fifth, economy, or the way to make money and save it. Sixth, morality, or the true knowledge of our relationship to God and our fellow man. These, I believe, will solve the problem of our present social condition. But to every ladder there are two sides upon which the steps must rest. In this social problem they are *protection* of rights and *equality* of rights.

The American idea in the minds of fifty millions of our white fellow citizens, must be educated to this, that we are human beings, or the problem never will be solved. The time must come when the colored American citizen must be given a chance in life, resting upon his own capacity to succeed. So long as we are deprived of this, we are not justly chargeable with thriftlessness; and the assertion of our inferiority of race is baseless and nonsensical. Above all let us ourselves not cease in the work of education, as a means of solving the Negro problem, for "Knowledge is power."

And now a word about our present political condition. This is not an unimportant topic, but space prevents me from saying but little. It is not so much what we have been politically, but what we are. It is known that in a large portion of our country the colored voter is virtually disfranchised, and that he finds no power in the constitution to protect him in the exercise of his ballot. Throughout the country he is only partially recognized in his rights as a citizen, to share in the administration of the government to which he owes allegiance. The chief reason of this is, that the Negro in politics has been too much of a *sentiment*. He needs to become more of a *reality*, and be found seeking his best interests. We must be students of politics, and no longer followers of other men's views. When it becomes necessary to change our party affiliations, do so like all free men the world over. But let our change be always to better our condition, otherwise "let well enough alone." Again, we must acknowledge leadership, and don't be all leaders.

Now, from all that I have stated, may I ask, What shall the future of the colored American be? I believe that, despite all the disadvantages which surround him, all obstacles now in his way, he will rise to a plane of unconceived excellence in manhood, in citizenship, in industry, in wealth, in education, and in moral standing, and become as polished columns in the temple of this great Republic. I predict that fifty years hence, when justice gets a foothold and is enthroned in the hearts of the American people of the Anglo-Saxon race, and history records the progress of races in art, literature, commerce, and industry, the verdict will be given the Negro of having attained a higher stage of civilization than any other race in a like period of time, and he will be found among the statesmen, poets, inventors, merchants, mechanics, artizans, authors, journalists, educators, agriculturalists, painters, capitalists, and all other civilized departments of our common country. We shall, in the future, continue to sit in the halls of legislation, and on the judicial bench, in the marts of commerce, and in places of industry, not as experiments, as heretofore, but as approved by all, because of our fitness and our capacity. We shall solve the race. problem by force of our worth, our intelligence, and our virtue. We shall not, as now, be tolerated, but accepted of our white brethren as equals in the North and in the South.

This is no dream, dear reader, nor is my plan Utopian, but out of the rude block, hewn out of the dark and dismal quarry of a cruel bondage, shall appear, by the chisel of education, and the polish of a wider intercourse with our more advanced brethren of the white race, supported by industry and money, and the benign influence of the genius of our republican institutions—the polished statue, of ebony in its hues, beautiful in symmetry of purpose, strong in unity of action, and lasting in the harmony of its structure; dressed in the full panoply of our rights as citizens, and girded with the strong sword of defence in equal and impartial laws, administered by non-partisan and pure judges, and in the light and enjoyment of political equality with all other citizens, seeking and possessing in the South both a free ballot and a fair count as a right; and in the North, East and West, exemplifying in the common engagement with other races in all the pursuits of life, our fitness and our capacity, and by our own strength in the mutual confidence, one in the other, enjoy a fuller inspiration of race pride and race possibilities. Thus shall we appear in the near future, aided by the expansion of the American idea of the common Fatherhood of God and the common brotherhood of man; and thus shall we be, out of many, one united people, indissoluble and unconquerable.

The time is coming when, in the arbitrament of contest now going on between capital and labor, we shall take a greater part than now. Just wages denied is a modified form of slavery. For two hundred and fifty years the labor of the slave has been for the benefit of another. Slavery has aided capital in its domination and tyranny over labor; and from no wages at all, we are but receiving enough to meet the wants of life in many sections of the country. The day of equality between labor, just wages and capital, is fast approaching. The equity of the Negro in labor in this contest must be decreed. He must, as he is entitled to, have a place in all industries. In order to achieve this position in the midst of opposition, race prejudice, low wages and social discrimination, he must Agitate! Educate! Co-operate! and Organize! "He who would be free, must the blow himself first strike."

CHAPTER X.

CONCLUSION.

If the foregoing views which I have given of the "New South" be suggestive only, they have attained their ends. No subject like this can be exhaustive. Whatsoever the new superstructure shall be, depends upon the reforms which I have indicated as necessary. That political party which gives to the South new life in giving to it new ideas, apace with the advancement of the age, will create a "New South," politically, morally, industrially, and socially. The greatest objection to the rapid advancement of the South is its political status. It is not within the purview of the constitution in its method of popular elections. The ultimate of continuing the method of disfranchisement of a large number of its citizens, will be to perpetuate, instead of annul, sectional strife, and to produce internecine strife. How can the North be expected to rest contented with being required to take twice as many votes to elect a representative of their own, as the South needs for the same purpose? When the illusion which now blinds the North disappears, such as formerly diverted the South from the issue between the right to extend slavery, and slavery itself, as an evil, it will be seen that the present method of political elections is subversive of all free government, just as much as slavery did.

If the South would realize the truth that

"On stepping stones of our dead selves,
We rise to higher things,"

it may do much toward its advancement. It cannot complain that the North has not shown it both clemency and favor, even to the loss of its (the North's) own rights. It remains to do its future work itself, modelled upon the grand plan declared by Abraham Lincoln, viz.: a "Government for the people, by the people, and of the people."

In nothing which I have written in the foregoing pages have I aught of malice or uncharitableness. During my stay in the South, in the State of South Carolina, I have enjoyed the friendship of many of my political opponents, so that if I had written altogether from personal experience, instead of observation and knowledge of others, I might have been able to give my picture of the South brighter shades in the recounting of events, but since history is, or should be, the impartial record of facts and the philosophy arising from the same, as reached by the author, I have been unable to do any more than give my personal views and suggestions of what I have seen and know.

The industrial development of the South, as shown in the former pages, gives great hope for a "New South" in the future. The millstone around its neck is its own method of solving its race and political difficulties. Contact is the method of assimilation unless the forces be repellant; hence the South, in its industrial progress by the introduction of Northern men and Northern money, must lose its old identity in its "New South," and in the next quarter of a century the "Old South" will disappear. Brotherly love will be its practice; equality of rights its trade mark, politically; friendship, its practice among all men and women of all races. This is a consummation devoutly wished for by the author of these pages, and nothing less will build up a "New South."

N. B.—The chapter on "Prominent Men of the Negro Race," as referred to in Preface, is omitted, owing to a want of space as prepared for. Reference is recommended to "Men of Mark" to supply this omission.

THE END.